ISBN: 9798423498320

ORLB05.5
First Edition, 2022

Published by Other Record Labels.

ISBN 9798423498320

www.otherrecordlabels.com

Get the Bonus Content

This book aims to demystify the process of creating an effective marketing strategy for your record label and your new releases. It is my hope that it provides more than enough to get you on your way to creating an impressive record label brand who releases music that gets heard.

I want to make sure that this book stays relevant and up to date. A lot of the resources and tools I mention in this book can be accessed in the link below.

Visit **otherrecordlabels.com/marketing-bonus** for extra resources to help you with marketing!

Be sure to join our private community of record labels at **http://facebook.otherrecordlabels.com**

Get more weekly advice on running a record label at **www.otherrecordlabels.com**

Record Label Marketing Strategies
*Simplified Strategies for Building A Record Label Brand
and Effectively Promoting Your New Releases*

Scott Orr

TABLE OF CONTENTS

PART THREE - **ARTIST AND RELEASE MARKETING**

Can I ask a quick favor??

The future impact of this book relies entirely on authentic <u>5 star reviews</u> on Amazon from readers like you!

If this book truly helps you, and if you want to support what I do, please consider heading over to Amazon and leaving a review of this book!

Simply go to **geni.us/recordlabelmarketing** (or use the QR code below) – this link will take you directly to my book on Amazon where you can leave a review!

Thank you so much!

- Scott

P.S. Never hesitate to reach out if there's anyway I can help you and your record label...
scott@otherrecordlabels.com

PART ONE
INTRODUCTION

INTRODUCTION

As a record label, there is no better feeling than discovering a new artist and finding ways to share their music with the world. The discovery and the creative processes that follow can be immensely exciting and rewarding. However, generating this attention and excitement among the public can feel daunting if not impossible, because of this, many record labels feel overwhelmed and fall short of their goals.

Through simple, day-to-day strategies, I believe you can make significant improvements in the way you build album campaigns, develop your label's brand, and promote your artists. It is through micro actions that you can see macro results.

Over the past several years, I have interviewed over 100 independent record labels of all sizes. I'm constantly amazed at how innovative and creative these labels are when it comes to how they promote their new releases and build their brands. In this book, my goal is to share some of these concepts with you. In addition to the lessons we learn from other record labels, I intend to share some of the things I've learned along the way, as a self-managed independent artist running my own record label.

There are traditional marketing strategies and more outside-the-box promotional tactics that I cover in this book. I have also included several resources for you and your team to help your record label succeed at promoting your new releases. At the end of each chapter, you will also find a "Quick Tip" to give you extra insights and hopefully something easy you can implement right away. Each chapter also includes a "Recommended" section where I highlight a helpful resource that will enhance your understanding of a given subject.

If I've done my job well, this book will offer a profitable and sustainable marketing model for your record label.

Let's get started!

BRAND MARKETING VS. ARTIST MARKETING

Before we dive into some didactic strategies, we need to understand the two categories of record label marketing: brand marketing and artist marketing. In most cases, the role of a record label is to help artists reach new listeners. However, there are unique times when a label must focus their promotional efforts on developing its own brand, separate from the individual artists. The chapters of this book are divided into these two subsets of record label (brand) marketing and artist (release) marketing.

Brand Marketing

The promotional strategies that create direct interactions and awareness with your record label is part of brand marketing. It is important to develop your label's own brand in parallel with the work you do for your artists. The influence and authority of your label can have a direct impact on the success of your artists.

Building a brand is simple, but it is not easy. It requires a long-term commitment to visual consistency, a generous attitude in the industry, and persistent dedication to doing right by your artists.

Audiences, artists, and members of the press will interact with your brand daily on social media, your website, and through in-person activities.

While it is important to develop your record label's brand, it is most important to ensure that you take a backseat to the needs of your artists, when necessary. Record labels exist to serve both the music fans and the music makers.

Artist Marketing

Each artist on your label's roster requires their own special promotional needs. They will all bring their own personal brand, audience, and aesthetic. This needs to be recognized and cultivated.

In most cases (and there have been exceptions), fans are more interested in the artists on the label than they are in the label itself. For this reason, a record label should prioritize organizing their artists' web presence, public image, and music catalog. Ultimately, their success will reflect positively on the record label.

PART TWO

RECORD LABEL BRAND MARKETING

CHAPTER ONE
DEFINING AND EMBRACING YOUR NICHE
Connecting your brand to a specific tribe of passionate fans.

The term "niche" is defined as a specialized segment of the market for a particular kind of product or service. A record label's niche could include their genre, geographic location, social stance, or any combination of specific categories.

The best way to define your niche is to start with the broadest audience category, and then start narrowing down with specifics: broad audience > niche > sub-niche. (Example: fitness instructor > fitness instructor for women > fitness instructor for pregnant women). For a record label, this niching-down tactic might look like this: record label > record label from Cleveland > punk record label from Cleveland.

There is no limit to how narrow you can go with your niche. Let's use the previous example and narrow the niche down even further: record label > record label from Cleveland > punk record label from Cleveland > all women, punk record label from Cleveland > vinyl only, all women, punk record label from Cleveland. As you can see, by defining your niche, you begin to define your audience.

The power of a narrow niche is in its ability to help fans identify with a brand that mirrors their personal tastes and values. You accomplish this by explicitly declaring who your label serves, doubling down on this ethos, and utilizing your niche to help you stand out from the crowd.

Here is how to create a narrow niche for your record label...

1. Defining Your Niche

To identify your own label's niche, you need to visualize your ideal customer avatar or the type of person you imagine to be most likely supporting and promoting your artists. Begin by listing as many unique characteristics as possible of this customer avatar. Include things like how old they are, where they're from, where they shop, what media they consume, what websites they visit, which social media platforms they use, how they listen to music, which local venues they frequent, what charities they support, and their personal values.

This list of specific characteristics will help you connect with an audience quicker than a record label that lacks such a unique identity. The vastness of the internet causes individuals to long for smaller, more intimate tribes. A well-defined niche helps consumers recognize brands and communities that share their interests and values.

Additionally, when defining your niche, try to identify an unmet need or underserved people group in your industry (e.g., Black artists in country music, modular synthesizers in classical music, musicians who are inmates and ex-offenders).

2. Embracing Your Niche

Your record label's niche is not simply an internal form of classification, it is an essential part of your external promotions. It is an identity that is recognized by the general public, not just you and your team. Declare your niche publicly on social media, your website, and at in-person events. Celebrate and boast about your niche by highlighting what makes your audience unique. Create specifically for it, sell merchandise that celebrates your community's identity, host relevant in-person events, and donate to causes that your fans are most passionate about.

3. Owning Your Niche

Your objective with identifying and embracing your record label's niche is to position your label as "one of one." By being specific in who you serve, you are creating a brand that stands alone, effectively eliminating the competition from a category that you defined. The goal for your record label is to become known for what you do, what you're about, and what you offer your audience.

Another benefit of owning a niche is that a niche provides your business with creative parameters. A clearly defined niche will help you stay focused on identifying what types of initiatives you should or shouldn't be investing in. A clearly defined niche should inform the A&R process in your search for new artists, it should dictate what types of physical formats you manufacture, and it should help craft your record label's messaging.

Do not hide your niche. Your newly defined niche should become your record label's motto or mission statement that you can use on your website and other branded materials. This will help future fans know they're in the right place!

Narrowing down your record label's niche may seem counterproductive; it may seem like you are alienating potential customers or excluding a broader audience.

While this may be true, the benefits of connecting with a passionate tribe far outweighs the downside to limiting your audience pool. You will notice that narrowing who your record label appeals to will create a more intimate connection with those within that specific group. These fans will be more likely to invest (financially and emotionally) in your label and your artists with conviction and passion.

Continue to narrow your focus on who your record label is meant to serve. Be a beacon for your people, and proudly embrace and celebrate what makes you and your community unique!

Quick Tip: *To define your own niche, start as broad as possible and begin to narrow. Be authentic in this process, choose descriptions and categories that mirror what you're passionate about, and what sets you apart from other labels. Try to narrow down your niche by at least 4 layers, to help you get as specific as possible.*

Layer 1: _____ > Layer 2: _____
> Layer 3:_____ > Layer 4:_____

(E.g. Layer 1: Independent Record Label > Layer 2: Independent Record Label featuring exclusively Detroit artists > Layer 3: Independent Lo-fi Jazz Record Label featuring exclusively Detroit artists > Layer 4: Independent Lo-fi Jazz Record Label featuring exclusively Detroit Black artists)

Here are a few examples of record labels who clearly define and promote their niche...

• Waxwork Records (US) - Specializing in releasing soundtracks and film scores of cult and genre movies exclusively on vinyl. (waxworkrecords.com)

• ATA Records (UK) - Authentic soul, funk, and jazz recorded in a vintage analogue studio, true to the era. (atarecords.co.uk)

• UMOR REX (Mexico) - Electronic atmospheres to avant-garde and other forms of experimental music with an impeccable emphasis on design and packaging. (umor-rex.com)

• Conviction Records (Scotland) - A record label for inmates of a Scottish prison. (instagram.com/convictionrecords)

CHAPTER TWO
UNDERSTANDING YOUR MARKET'S SOPHISTICATION

Effectively communicating with an overexposed audience.

It is important that you appreciate how sophisticated your audience of music fans truly are. Simply put, understanding market sophistication means that your record label understands exactly how familiar your audience is with the type of product you are selling. It also considers how desensitized your market might be to the types of marketing that is common in your industry. For example, the simple act of an independent artist releasing an EP on Spotify often feels ignored by the public. This is because it is no longer the novel accomplishment it may have been in the past. The sophistication of your audience simply means they are harder to impress.

Acknowledging and understanding this concept of market sophistication will help you develop marketing strategies that are unorthodox, original, and innovative. It should help you avoid lazy or overused promotional tactics. A record label isn't automatically entitled to an attentive audience, that is something you must earn.

Customers aren't beholden to your company unless you have something novel and exciting, something that provides value.

Here are a few ways you can communicate with a sophisticated audience...

1. Highlighting Your Unique Selling Point

The simplest way to elevate the communication with your audience is to clearly state your label's unique selling point. Fans have endless options when it comes to finding new music, it is important that when they find you, they know why and how your label is special. This can be easily accomplished by declaring your value statement on your website, social media bios, or through your label's regular communications.

2. Creating Meaningful Connections

In today's economy, consumers demand more meaningful connections. Purchases are no longer simply transactional; they are expected to be transformative.

Therefore, your emphasis needs to shift from whatever the widget is or what it does, to how it contributes to the identity and ideals of the end user. Put simply, how does what you do as a record label directly impact people's lives?

You can accomplish this style of marketing by focusing on the results instead of the features.

This can be done by strategically communicating the feelings and emotions your listeners receive when experiencing your releases, or by highlighting the impact that their financial contribution has on the lives of the artists they love.

At the very least, you showcase your label's identity by way of a cohesive aesthetic of your releases, a consistent genre, or a commitment to your local geographic region.

3. Maximizing Transparency

I was interviewing a record label owner not too long ago who was telling me about the various complaints they receive from customers who order vinyl from their store. Some of the complaints centered around shipping costs, pre-order delays, or why they weren't pressing more vinyl once a record has sold out. During this conversation, we realized that the problem wasn't with the label, nor was it an issue of an entitled customer. The problem stemmed from the fact that most music fans don't know how the music industry works. Hence, when they see a vinyl record priced at $40, with an international shipping cost of $25, they'll assume the record label is greedy, or at best, out of touch. Open communication and transparency will help enlighten your customers to the challenges that come with running a record label. Don't assume they know how everything works; they don't live and breathe this industry like you do. Be empathetic and compassionate to their lack of understanding and find unique ways where you can educate them in a non-patronizing way. Show them how everything works, dispel myths, be forthcoming about manufacturing costs, supply chain issues, or shipping charges that are out of your control.

A record label that is aware of their market's sophistication is a label that can create more impactful and empathetic products. You'll be able to communicate the significant impact of the artist/fan relationship more effectively, and you should always be looking for ways to develop and nurture that relationship.

Find ways to clarify and communicate what makes your label unique in the music industry. Bring your customers into the experience of making music, enlighten them of how record labels operate, and the role they play in an artist's career.

In the music industry, the audience doesn't really care about the utility of a piece of music. Instead, they define value in terms of emotions, how the music makes them feel. For this reason, record labels must strive to connect on a more personal level with their audience, to focus less on the features (vinyl colors, recording quality, vanity metrics) and focus more on the feeling the art invokes.

Quick Tip: *Avoid being patronizing or pedantic to your audience. Understand that, unlike you, they don't live in the weeds of the music industry daily. Be empathetic to their desire to enjoy great music and support the artists they love.*

There's a label called, This and That Tapes from Philadelphia who has an extremely novel way of distributing digital music. When a customer purchases a cassette tape off them, they include a "digital rip" of the cassette. This means that the label has undergone the arduous task of digitally recording the playback of the actual cassette tape. These digital audio files now have the "sound" of playing a tape, but with the convenience of an mp3. It is a unique way to distribute music digitally, and it's something I've never seen done before!

CHAPTER THREE
IMPROVING YOUR RECORD LABEL'S WEB PRESENCE

Monitoring and maintaining your label's online activity.

An independent record label's web presence can often be disjointed, out-of-date, inconsistent, and disorganized. The solution is to optimize and unify your web properties (social media, website, artists' websites) to share a common goal. In this chapter, we'll discuss how to implement small fixes and tweaks that add up to make a big impact on your fans' experience with your record label online.

Let's look at three ways we can bring value to our audience...

1. Choosing a Primary Destination

It is important that you create a content hierarchy for your web presence. You are not being a helpful guide to your audience when you attempt to equally prioritize all options and initiatives at once. Your website shouldn't give equal prominence to your newest release, back catalog albums, merch items, and social media links. Instead, you need to clearly show them where to go, what is most important, and what comes secondary if they decide to stay longer. Too many equally ranked options will paralyze your visitors. If you confuse people, you lose people!

To find what your primary objective is for your visitors, you need to ask yourself, what is the most important and/or impactful action for your audience? Is it related to revenue? Do you want them to follow you on Twitter, or subscribe to your YouTube channel? Determine what action-step produces the greatest return for your record label, and then make it clear to your visitors that this is the most important button they should click. As an example, for a lot of businesses an email list produces the greatest return and captures the most value from a web visitor. That is why you see prominent headlines that invite visitors to sign up to a mailing list in exchange for a free download, discount code, or a similar lead magnet. In this example, the company will ensure that a "Join Now" button is most prominent on their site and that it is enticing to sign up.

Finally, ensure that all your links (link in bio, web banners, ads, email signature, etc.) point to this primary destination.

2. Planned Sustainability

An out-of-date website is worse than no website at all. It is important that you create web properties that are easy to maintain, self-sustaining, and evergreen. Be careful when implementing blog features or news sections that require constant attention to stay relevant.

Eliminate any sections of your web presence that require frequent maintenance but produce low engagement. You can even eliminate entire platforms (TikTok, Instagram, etc.) that have become too overwhelming for you to manage consistently.

Furthermore, conduct a weekly or monthly audit of your websites to ensure that everything is up to date. Look for banners with expired dates, dead links, typos, events that have passed, or content that is no longer relevant.

3. Cross-Platform Consistency

Lastly, aim for a cohesive visual aesthetic across all your properties. Use the same logo, tagline, brand colors, and username across the various social media platforms. This simple step will help your audience easily discover your record label on all the various sites around the web.

In the early stages of running a record label, it will be impossible for you to maintain a comprehensive and multi-faceted web presence. Keep it simple by directing visitors to a singular, primary destination that produces the best results for your record label. Eliminate any unnecessary or time-consuming pages that are prone to neglect. Finally, creating a visual aesthetic – delicately threaded through all your web properties – will help your audience stay connected and engaged.

Quick Tip: *If you're just getting started, a fully fleshed out website isn't necessary. A placeholder webpage or utilizing an existing platform as your main web page can suffice until you are ready to build a long-term option. However, I do suggest that you purchase the domain name that you eventually wish to use. You can "point" this domain to a temporary site like your record label's Bandcamp page, a blog, or even your Instagram account.*

Visit as many record label websites as you can in one hour. Then, make a list of consistent features or layouts that you found helpful as a visitor. Conversely, make a list of elements that frustrated you or made the website unnecessarily difficult to navigate.

CHAPTER FOUR
PROVIDING VALUE TO FANS
A deeper look into why fans choose to support artists and labels.

Most of our spending as individuals happens at the subconscious level. We aren't generally aware of the deeper meanings behind why we buy what we buy or why we value certain objects, memberships, or pieces of information.

I believe it is because these things help us establish our identities. We buy certain clothes to show people what type of person we are. We read books that help us become who we hope to become. We donate to charities and organizations that share the same morals and values as we do. These products help us outwardly display our internal identities and values.

I don't mean to be overly philosophical, but I think the things we purchase are more connected to our identity than we care to believe. For this reason, record labels need to position themselves in a way that helps fans understand why supporting your artists or buying a t-shirt can bring value to their lives. I'm not suggesting that a piece of band merch is equivalent to a loaf of bread, I'm simply encouraging you to look deeper into how your record label can provide meaningful value to your fans.

This can be done by attaching your label to a

meaningful cause, reinforcing the idea of enabling creatives, or simply creating beautiful products. Record labels provide their community with value by creating products that contribute to a fan's desired lifestyle.

Let's look at three ways we can bring value to our audience...

1. Designing With Empathy

Our products have a better chance of making an impact on people's lives when we design with empathy. User-centered design is a process that pays close attention to a user's feelings, needs, and emotions. Record labels can implement an empathetic design process by releasing products that effectively resonate with their community. Learn what excites your audience and what repels them. Embrace technology that compliments their lifestyle and produce products that contribute to their aesthetic, ethics, and preferences.

Based out of Chicago, Trouble in Mind Records is a label that intentionally prices their vinyl records under $20 when possible. Owner Bill Roe told me, back when he worked as a clerk in a record store, he would see customers peruse the store with an armful of albums. However, when it came time to check out, they were forced to narrow their selection down to only one or two records. Based on his observations, Bill set out to price his label's releases at a lower price point, to allow customers to afford more music. This is an example of empathetic design. Creating affordable products greatly benefits their fans. This helps create a symbiotic relationship between the record label and the music buyer, one that is built on awareness and empathy.

2. Standing for Something

Record labels who attach themselves to a cause (amplifying marginalized voices, empowering creatives, serving their community, climate action) are more likely to have a stronger connection with their audience. Today, fans are looking for brands that are more than just a logo. They want to support ideas and ethics. The relationship between a brand and a customer has become more personal, more than simply a transaction.

Fans are more likely to support your record label if they know who and what they are supporting. I was recently speaking with a special record label from the Philippines called Kadasig (otherrecordlabels.com/other-record-labels-blog/kadasig-interview). Their purpose is to assist in preserving and redefining the traditional language of Bisaya. Fans not only enjoy supporting this label because the music is great (CNN Philippines added one of their songs to their best songs of 2021 list), but they also find satisfaction in knowing they are helping promote and preserve their culture.

You must find something to stand for as a record label. Do you share a common enemy with your audience (e.g., discrimination, inequality, environmental waste, gatekeepers)? What is your community most passionate about? These are the kind of things your audience wants to hear from you.

3. Highlighting the End Result

Spotify has a playlist called "Stay in Bed" that contains songs that are meant to inspire the listener to relax, de-stress, and to... stay in bed. For the sake of argument, let's call this playlist a "product." In this example, what is the result for the customer who listens to this playlist? The reward this product is offering is permission to relax, take the day off, and be comfortable.

Similarly, what is the end-result of someone buying a new mattress? A good night's sleep, of course. Therefore, advertisers tend to focus on the "end result" when promoting a product or service. Home Depot's slogan is "you can do it, we can help" which signifies to potential customers that their home improvement dreams are doable, and their brand is the one to help them accomplish it.

So, what is the end-result of someone supporting your artists? What is their reward for buying a record from you? I may be being dramatic, but I want to express the need for record labels to emphasize the benefits of their products, not just the features.

Customers want to feel good about giving away their money. Today, transactions have become more than an impersonal exchange. Instead, fans expect their purchases to reflect their values, ethics, and to support their chosen lifestyle. While some of this may sound superficial, it teaches us to promote products on a deeper level. It teaches us to talk about the benefits, not just the features. When you position your record label as socially conscious and empathetic, you create a special bond with your supporters.

Quick Tip: *Interact with your audience. Embed yourself in the community of your record label. Spend time at in-person events, on online message boards, and industry organizations. Connect with your customers via email and through social media. Find out what types of products and content that they enjoy the most. While it is true that record labels are curators – presenting previously undiscovered art to the world – it is also true that we need to listen to our audience and find out how we can strengthen the bond between fan and artist, customer, and record label.*

Speaking of designing with empathy, check out the book, *Well Designed* by John Kolko to help you better grasp the meaning behind creating things that bring meaning to people's lives. (otherrecordlabels.com/books)

CHAPTER FIVE
CREATING PERSONAL CONNECTIONS WITH YOUR FANS

Creating intimate interactions with your audience.

We live in an increasingly digital world and the music community is no exception. Industry professionals, fans, and artists alike are looking for ways to intimately connect with each other. This reality presents an interesting opportunity for record labels to act as a bridge builder between musicians and listeners. As a record label, there can be some incredible ways for record labels to weld a connection between the digital and tangible world.

While what I'm saying may sound obvious, it's easier said than done. Most of our interactions with artists and fans occur online through email, social media, message boards, or YouTube. The ease and ubiquity of communication technology makes it more arduous to connect on a personal level with your audience.

The record labels who strive to connect on a deeper level with their fans can experience more engagement, higher revenue, and more meaningful relationships with their supporters.

Here are some simple ways you can create personal, real-life connections with your customers...

1. Make it Physical

The best way to bring our online relationships offline is through physical media. When a fan orders a record from your label, use this opportunity to include bonus items that surprise and delight your customers. Shipping mailers and boxes are often wasted opportunities for record labels to overdeliver. Use these opportunities to include record label stickers, printed download codes, candy, bonus 7" records, overstock, or a label compilation CD.

At the very least, a personal note to the customer can go a long way. Such a simple act can create an intimate bond with the fan that may result in more sales, referrals, and social engagement.

You don't even have to wait for a physical order to reach out to your audience, gather mailing addresses from previous orders or ask for your artists if they have their own mailing lists. Mail a Christmas letter, postcard, or zine. Find ways where you can break the online barrier to create a more intimate connection with your audience.

2. Making it Authentic

There are many ways for your record label to show your identity to your audience. Don't be afraid to use social media or your mailing list to share your personal story, declare your allegiance to a noble cause, or represent your country or your genre. Be clear and explicit about who you are as a record label and what you stand for. Give updates on the status of the label, be honest about your needs as well as financial limitations. Use social media to show your fans insights into your personal life or behind the scenes at your label.

You could also start a podcast about your record label and talk about a different artist each episode or a different era of your label's journey. Use unique platforms to authentically communicate with your community.

Another way to showcase authenticity is to allow your fans a peek behind the curtain at your label's operations or your artists' creative process. Behind the scenes content is exhilarating for fans. Give your audience a chance to see how records are made, a look at an average day at a record label, or inside a manufacturing plant. Not only will this create quality content for you to share with your audience, it will also help them be more empathetic and understanding at how involved running a record label can be.

3. Make it Personal

Dale Carnegie said, "A person's name is to that person, the sweetest, most important sound in any language." Take the time for the human element of running a record label. Use their real names in emails or on social media, send your fans personal thank-you notes with their orders, or even email them out of the blue telling them how much you appreciate their support. Stay in touch with your audience, even when you have nothing to sell.

There's a silly trend in the music industry where small companies try to appear larger than they are. They use "we" instead of "I" or they default to a general mailbox instead of using a personal email. There may come a time where anonymity is essential to your business, but don't be unnecessarily impersonal with your fans.

The more we force ourselves out of our comfort zone, the more we grow as record labels. Strong relationships are formed through meaningful interactions and moments of authenticity. Look for ways that your label can create offline connections with your fans. Overdeliver to your customers when it's appropriate and sustainable. Finally, be sure you are clearly and authentically expressing your values with your audience on a regular basis.

Some of these acts are small, while some are slightly more involved, but the goal remains the same, to create personal connections with the members of your record label's community.

Quick Tip: *Place an order with a handful of other independent record labels. Review their purchasing process and see what parts of the process you enjoy as a music fan. When the order arrives, observe what they include (or don't include) and evaluate what bonuses you enjoyed as a fan, and where you think they may have missed an opportunity to overdeliver.*

Check out a great book on this topic called *Superfans* by entrepreneur and business expert, Pat Flynn.

CHAPTER SIX
UTILIZING UNIQUE GUERRILLA MARKETING TECHNIQUES
Non-traditional marketing strategies to help you reach a wider audience.

Guerrilla marketing is a marketing strategy that uses surprise, spontaneity, and unconventional interactions to promote a product. Some now-familiar examples of guerrilla marketing are flash mobs, staged arguments, treasure hunts, reverse graffiti (using pressure washing), among other unique publicity stunts.

The term, "Guerrilla Marketing" was coined back in 1984 by author Jay Conrad Levinson. Today, we might simply call it "viral marketing." The pursuit of going viral is ubiquitous in modern social advertising, something many strive for, but few achieve. You can predict what may or may not go viral as much as you can predict the stock market.

Social media virality simply means that your tactic has worked, and your message is resonating with people. Sometimes records or artists themselves go viral based on talent alone. Unfortunately, that isn't the norm, and modern marketing requires more unconventional ideas.

In addition to the traditional marketing strategies, we'll discuss in this book, your record label should develop outside-the-box promotional plans that separate you from everyone else. Traditional platforms

(Facebook, YouTube, TikTok) are crowded communities of competing voices. Truly innovative labels are the ones who create their own platforms, and who create unique ways to reach new listeners.

Here are a few outside-the-box marketing strategies your label can implement...

1. Engaging with Less-utilized Promo Outlets

Recently, I found a few Instagram accounts that showcased inspiring examples of graphic design. These accounts boasted a few hundred thousand followers who all enjoy a daily dose of design inspiration. I reached out to them and submitted the artwork from a recent album campaign on my label. To my surprise, most of them charged a nominal repost fee ($25-$50), which was fine and seemed fair. This was an interesting experiment for my label as it provided an opportunity to get our album cover in front of a few hundred thousand creatives. The results were great, a handful of new followers and a few album sales. But that's not why I mention this experiment.

The principle of this experiment was finding a way to promote a release in an online community with less competition than traditional music sites. In fact, my post was the only album cover this account had posted in the previous three months!

Every record label and DIY artist is submitting their album to The FADER, Rolling Stone, UPROXX, or Pitchfork. Far fewer artists are utilizing other influencers or outlets. This opens up an opportunity for us to engage with lesser-utilized platforms.

Reach out to non-music blogs to pitch your music. Find communities of like-minded individuals: submit songs to yoga blogs, sell your records in a local tattoo parlor, license tracks to YouTubers, or curate a playlist for a local coffee shop.

2. Going Offline

The internet and social media have created incredible opportunities for artists and labels to reach previously unreachable audiences. At the same time, it seems everyone is competing for the same audience. All the while the competition for people's attention has significantly increased. Furthermore, social media has caused a lot of companies to become lazy in their marketing efforts, failing to create intimate engagement with their audiences. The solution is to go offline more often.

Find ways to promote your artists and releases in your local record store (live performances, window posters, giveaways), set-up a booth at local festivals and fairs, mail letters/postcards to previous customers with an exclusive coupon code. One record label I spoke with from Ohio (Refresh Records) told me they once set-up a booth at a local flea market, selling (a lot of) records and t-shirts!

3. **Empowering Your Fans**

Another surefire way to get your fans engaged with your brand is to "pass them the ball." Ask questions on social media, post weekly challenges, or ask for direct feedback from your audience. People will feel more connected to your artists and your label if you involve them on a more interactive level. The fan/record label relationship is often only one-way, look for opportunities that allow your fans to interact with you in fun and engaging ways.

In addition to utilizing traditional marketing tools, look for ways that your record label can stand out from the crowd by implementing unconventional promotions.

As you experiment with new, non-traditional promotional ideas, keep track of your efforts and their results in a spreadsheet or a journal. This will help you know what initiatives are worth implementing again on future campaigns.

Guerrilla marketing can create an instantaneous, intimate connection with an audience through low-cost, unconventional strategies that utilize the element of surprise, humor, convenience, emotion, and passion.

Instead of sitting in traffic with your promotional efforts, veer off and find an alternate route for you and your artists. Outside-the-box marketing techniques can help differentiate your releases from the others.

It is incredibly hard to get our releases heard. Successful record labels are the ones who create their own unique ways for their music to be heard. Try something that has never been done before!

Quick Tip: *Today's audience has become a little bit fatigued to atypical marketing tactics, especially if they can be spotted as intentionally unconventional. The idea of guerrilla marketing is to surprise and delight your audience, this has to be accomplished authentically, otherwise it can have the opposite effect. Audiences are extremely sophisticated and don't like being tricked. Effective "viral" campaigns are hard to come by, they're usually preceded by a trail of failed, cringe-worthy attempts. Tread lightly on this terrain. Don't underestimate or patronize your audience!*

I've compiled a few more outside-the-box marketing ideas on a checklist you can read at the back of the book.

CHAPTER SEVEN
UNDERSTANDING THE BASICS OF WEB SEO
Search engine optimization for record labels.

Building a successful business consists of discovering your audience, nurturing your audience, and delivering to your audience. The way a lot of people will discover your record label is through a search engine. For this reason, SEO (or Search Engine Optimization) is key to ensuring that you remove barriers that may prevent people from discovering your label.

SEO is a complicated subject, and I don't plan on getting overly technical. Having said that, there are a few simple things you can do to improve your discoverability.

Here are the three types of SEO that you should become familiar with...

1. Brand SEO

This type of SEO is the easiest to succeed at and should be your top priority. Simply put, brand SEO is ensuring that your website (or web properties) show up in the top of the search results when someone searches for your actual brand name. This is an extremely critical part of SEO because it means someone is searching for your label by typing in your label's name.

For example, a label name like Sub Pop Records is extremely unique and therefore would very easily dominate the first page of search results. Whereas, if your label name is "Family Records" then you are going to have a much harder time competing against search results for genealogy websites, etc.

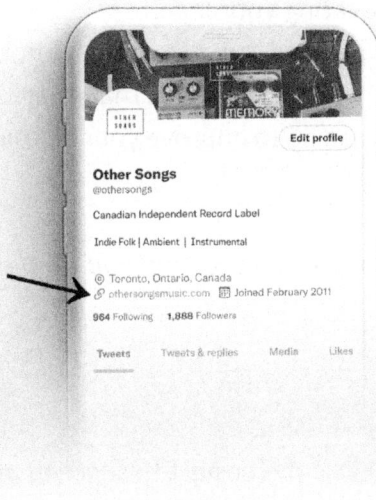

Whether your label name is generic or highly unique, it is important that you make sure your name is consistent across all social media platforms and on your home page. Additionally, include your main URL in the bio section of your profile on all your social media platforms. This consistency will help Google (and other search engines) easily identify the similarities, and successfully link each web platform to the same search result. The goal is to occupy a handful of first page results when someone searches your brand name. For example, If you search "Sub Pop" into Google, the label dominates all five search results on the first page. The search results include Sub Pop's official website, Wikipedia page, Twitter account, YouTube channel, and their Facebook page.

A lot of fans will use Google to find your label or to quickly find your social media platforms, Bandcamp page, or Soundcloud. For this reason, brand SEO should be a top priority for your record label.

2. Localized SEO

Localized SEO is when we work to ensure fans can find us by searching through relevant regional and geographic search terms. For example, if you are a record label from Detroit, you want listeners to come across your label when they search for "Detroit record labels." This is mostly applicable to more localized regions as opposed to entire countries. This means you should aim to have your record label show up in the first few pages of search results when people search for your city or town name plus the term "record label."

This may not be a high priority when it comes to record label SEO, however sometimes fans want to support labels who are from their hometown. Or perhaps a tour promoter is looking for a local opening act. There may even be cases where music supervisors are looking for artists who are from a specific region.

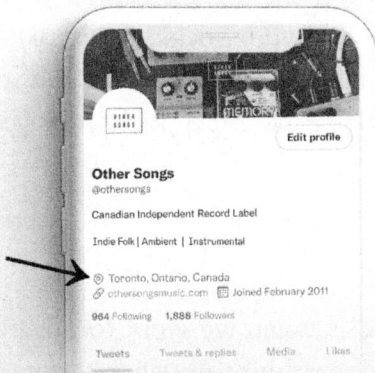

A simple way to optimize your web properties for local and regional consideration is to include

CREATIVE TIPS & IDEAS

your city/location name in all of your profiles on social media. Register your record label location (office, studio, home office) on Google Maps, and with your local arts online directories. Finally, another way to help Google identify our geographic connection is to include your location in a headline on your website. For example, on your home page, use a top-level headline that says something like, "The Newest Hip-Hop Label in Detroit."

3. **Topical SEO**

This kind of SEO pertains mostly to the primary genre of your record label. On your website, you should include your genre (or unique identity) in the headline or page title. For example, New Hope Records: Detroit's Newest Hip-Hop Record Label. In this example, you've used your label name (brand SEO), your geographic location (localized SEO), as well as your genre (topical SEO). Adopting a niche sub-genre is another great way to increase your chances of being discovered by relevant fans. Be sure to include keywords that signal to a potential fan that your label is relevant to their tastes.

If there is something unique to your record label, make sure you consistently use that across your website descriptions, social media bios, and in the hashtags you use. This will help search engines connect your record label to these topics.

SEO is not something you need to spend too much time worrying about in the early stages of your record label. Nor does it make or break a release campaign. Although, maintaining consistency with your marketing copy across your various web properties will go a long way in helping improve your record label's SEO.

Quick Tip: *A lot of modern web design platforms have robust, built-in SEO features. Companies like Squarespace (otherrecordlabels.com/squarespace), Shopify, or WIX will offer user-friendly tools that make it easy for you to manage your SEO. Eventually, you'll want to grow to the level where you can hire a company or an employee to manage your web properties and optimize your site for search.*

For a deeper dive into the subject of SEO, check out the book, *Product-Led SEO* by Eli Schwartz.

CHAPTER EIGHT
A SUSTAINABLE SOCIAL MEDIA STRATEGY
Developing a social media strategy for your record label.

Social media isn't for everyone. You're lucky if you or someone who works for your record label is specialized in this constantly demanding space. Most of us struggle with populating our social media channels on a regular basis. Not only that, but it can be hard to keep up with the ever-changing relevance of various platforms. Trends change, algorithms evolve, and user engagement will ebb and flow without notice.

The simple solution is to develop a sustainable content strategy that you or a member on your team can easily maintain. Consistency is paramount when it comes to social media. It generates trust, brand awareness, and it helps content creators stay organized.

In this chapter, I want to propose a simple communication strategy that I've developed and utilized, not only with my own record label, but with any business I work with. The framework is made up of the four types of content that you might share with your audience: daily interactions, weekly content, monthly offers, and quarterly products. This framework maximizes the relationship between quality and quantity. For example, daily interactions (tweets, emails) are easy to create and are therefore more frequently utilized. Whereas something like a product (new album, new merch items) are more arduous to develop and are therefore something labels are not able to release as often.

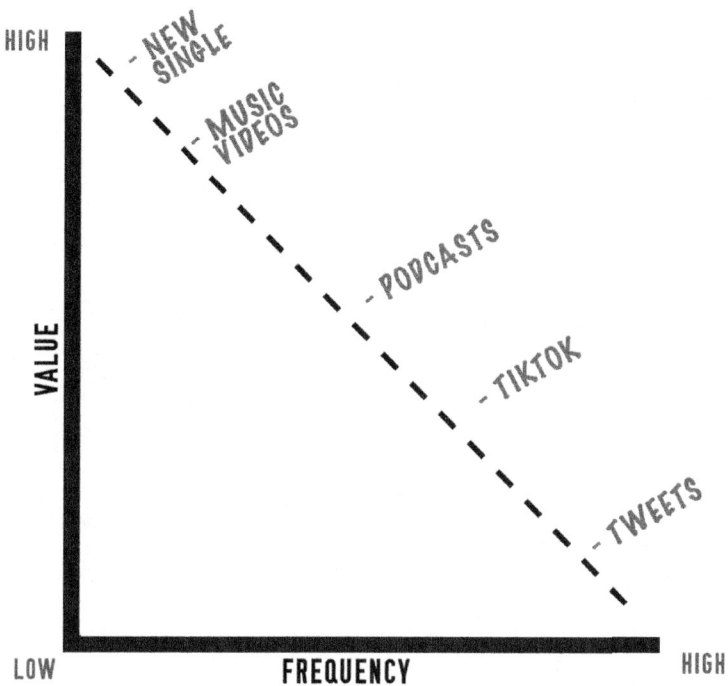

Here are the differences between the four types of content...

1. Daily Interactions

Daily interactions consist of easy-to-achieve, low value content such as tweets, Instagram stories, website content, industry emails, fan interactions, etc. These may not generate excitement from your audience, but they are essential to maintain brand awareness and audience engagement.

2. Weekly Content

An example of weekly content would be something more involved that you produce once a week. This can include blog posts, podcast episodes, YouTube vlog, or a well-planned TikTok video. For an artist, this type of content may be a B-side, a cover song, live performance, or a media appearance. Even something as simple as a video update can help fans feel connected to the artists they enjoy.

3. Monthly Offer

A monthly offer is a scheduled opportunity to bless your audience. Things like seasonal sales on your web store, pre-order launch, or a promotional campaign that highlights a back catalog release. It is helpful if this piece of content is free. You can produce a helpful resource, collaborate with another organization, or take part in a charitable cause. A free (or generous) offer can help generate reciprocity between both parties.

4. Quarterly Product

Finally, the most infrequent, yet high-valued piece of content is a product. This can be a new album, a label compilation, or a new line of merch. This can also be a time when you launch a new initiative like a YouTube channel, a Patreon, or a new record label podcast. This should be a revenue-generating initiative, something that contributes to the sustainability of your record label. Reserving your product/initiative release to only four times a year will help prevent your fans from feeling fatigued by too many product promotions.

As you can see, these four types of content will help you strategize how and when you release new products, initiatives, online sales, and fan interactions.

This simple strategy can be utilized by both the record label and the artist. Record labels should be populating their social media channels on a consistent and strategic basis, even when you don't have a new release to promote. Similarly, artists are advised to stay in contact with their audience year-round, and to develop a loyal following. Artists can share demos, in-studio photos, travel photos, and artist commentary episodes. Some artists don't enjoy social media or are concerned that it may affect their creativity. In some cases, they may just need to be encouraged to find the right platform that compliments their personality. Other times, they need protection and support when they are feeling pressured by the constant demands of social media.

Quick Tip: *Having a content asset management system in place will help you keep track of your social media content inventory. Store photos, videos, lyrics, production notes, and behind-the-scenes content in a centralized location like Dropbox or a Google Drive. This content can then be quickly utilized and repurposed for social media. For example, the same video you post on TikTok or Instagram Reels can also be used as a Canvas on Spotify for a new single.*

Check out our micro-course on this subject, taught by music publicist Jamie Coletta: *Social Media for Record Labels* **(otherrecordlabels.com/microcourses)**

CHAPTER NINE
UTILIZING EMAIL MARKETING
How to effectively use this enduring marketing tool.

One of the most underrated tools in a marketer's arsenal isn't a trending new app or social platform. Email marketing may lack some of the flashy appeal and vanity metrics of social media, but it remains one of the most effective ways to reach your audience. According to Oberlo (Source: oberlo.ca/blog/email-marketing-statistics), 4 billion people use email, with two thirds of subscribers happily receiving emails once a week from the brands they enjoy.

A person's inbox is far more personal and intimate than their social media feed. People are accustomed to receiving important emails in their inbox (government forms, company receipts, family updates) and are therefore more likely to carefully monitor what gets delivered. Things that happen on social media rarely hold this level of importance, resulting in users mindlessly scrolling through their feeds with little concern for what they're seeing.

Building an authentic email list of supporters, customers, and fans will provide your label with a trustworthy and profitable channel of communication.

The beauty of an email list is that you own it, and it is (generally) void of those pesky algorithms. You can build and nurture your list over many years, regardless of what social platforms come in and out of vogue.

*Here are three things to know when creating an email
marketing strategy...*

1. Start Capturing Emails

Before a fan will give you their email, you first
need to give them something of value. A transaction must take place. Most folks are hesitant
to give away their email address, it is a precious and protected asset. This is a good thing;
it means they pay attention to the emails that
show up in their inbox.

To get started, use a free service like Mailchimp
or Constant Contact to create a "landing page."
A landing page is a single page website with a
clear offer (e.g., "Enter your email for a chance
to win a free CD") and a form field for them to
enter their email. Once they submit their email
address, they should be taken to a page (of your
choosing) where they are given their free content (or a confirmation of entry).

Lead magnets (the download or content you offer potential subscribers in exchange for their
email) can be things like free downloads, un-

released material, contest entries, exclusive videos, or any type of digital content you think offers enough incentive for visitors to part with their precious email address.

While landing pages are most effective at converting visitors to subscribers, at the very least, ensure you have a simple pop-up form embedded on your website that invites people to "sign up to your mailing list." Keep in mind, this option is a last resort, without any clear incentive, most visitors will not enter their email address willingly.

2. Create a Sustainable Email Schedule

I would recommend monthly emails as the most sustainable schedule for small to medium size record labels. Weekly emails are far more audacious, and you are likely setting yourself up to fail. Weekly emails require a lot of content and a lot of commitment. Instead, pick an email frequency that is sustainable for your record label.

In fact, ensure that you choose a frequency that is sustainable for you over the long term. Weekly emails should be reserved for record labels who have a large roster and can safely generate quality content every week. A monthly schedule is a more sustainable frequency for most independent labels.

3. Build a Label List AND an Artist List

Nurturing an email list for your record label's audience is a great way to stay connected with your fans. However, you should also be aiming to build separate mailing lists for each one of your artists. While artists email lists may be smaller, they should be more direct and relevant, and will likely have a more successful open rate (the percentage of subscribers who open a specific email out of the total number of subscribers on your mailing list). In addition to building a global email list for your record label, you should also assist your artists in building their own email list that they can take with them should they move on from the label.

Email is powerful, and it doesn't seem to be going anywhere anytime soon. Do not overlook the value of building and nurturing a healthy email list for your record label.

Quick Tip: *Don't waste time worrying about unsubscribers. A lot of brands email their subscribers more than once a week. In fact, according to Benchmark, a third of all brands email their list 3-5 times each week. A more conservative schedule of weekly or monthly emails will unlikely annoy your audience. Having said that, it is okay if people do choose to unsubscribe, they were never going to support you in the first place. If at all possible, try to avoid looking at your unsubscribe numbers, they will only upset you. The truth is, unsubscribing is a natural pruning process, ensuring we are only reaching out to folks who want to hear from us.*

My favorite book that covers email marketing is *The 1-Page Marketing Plan* by Alan Dib. Visit **otherrecordlabels.com/books** for information on how to grab a copy.

CHAPTER TEN
THE FACE AND NAME OF YOUR RECORD LABEL

Utilizing the human element to connect with your audience.

In the late 1800s and early 1900s, a record label was a company that made phonographs (record players, or more recently turntables). They owned the technology to mechanically play records and therefore were the ones who would manufacture the rotating discs containing sound recordings. The more of these sound recordings they sold, the more people would buy their record players. And so, the first record labels were manufacturing companies who were manufacturing machines and records to play on those machines.

The reason for this brief history lesson is to show how unrelatable these early "record labels" were. There was no aesthetic, genre affiliation, or unique personality to these labels. They were historically unfriendly to artists, exploitative, and uninterested in establishing a unique sonic "vibe" that we would later see in independents like Motown, Sun Records, or Blue Note. They were simply manufacturing companies who wanted to sell machines.

As the patents for records expired, more independent record labels began to emerge. This time, these new record labels weren't making machines, they were music companies interested in signing, recording, and selling music from talented artists. They were real people with a real passion for music makers and music fans!

This is where *our* story begins. Modern independent record labels in the 2000s, 2010s, 2020s operate with a new set of ground rules. We exist as an alternative to an industry that is no longer relevant to today's music fans. For this reason, it is vital that your record label proudly displays your passion and purpose.

Here are a few ways you can create a unique identity for your record label...

1. Acting in the First Person

There's this common trend where solopreneur business owners talk like they're running a multi-staff corporation. "We're so excited to show you what we're about to release, we think you're going to love it!"

This happens with record labels too! Small record labels try to appear already-established, mysterious, and unapproachable. This is a fool's errand! Today's audiences are far too sophisticated for this type of grandstanding. Music fans prefer interacting with real people, they appreciate authenticity and they're looking for a personality to connect with who shares their same interests and values.

Use your real name when interacting with fans via email or on social media. Upload a picture of yourself to your website so fans can see what the label owner looks like. Share behind-the-scenes photos of your label operations and interactions with your artists. It is important that your audience knows who you are and what you stand for. Customers want to buy from people, not from companies.

2. Creating a Mission Statement

Mission statements can be inspiring and guiding, they can be a public display of values, or they can be an internal dedication. A meaningful mission statement should express your record label's goals and how it plans to achieve them. This should ultimately be your reason for existing, written out on paper. It should be shared with your artists, staff members, and in some cases, your audience as well.

Just before you start to create a mission statement, ensure you understand the "why" behind your record label's existence. Clearly outline what drives you internally. What is the macro reason behind your micro ambitions?

A powerful mission statement should be made up of a few tangible and explicit goals. Outline three or four philosophical goals that are important to you and that align with the mission of your record label. Explicit goals can be things like maintaining healthy relationships with your artists, having a positive impact on your local arts community, or creating a safe space for artists from marginalized groups.

3. Adopting a Purpose

There's a great quote that's often attributed to Malcom X that says, "if you don't stand for something, you'll fall for anything." This idea shows us the importance of adopting a purpose for our lives, and in this case, our record label. It shows us how having focus can help us, not only achieve our goals, but it also trains us to ignore competing distractions.

Here's a helpful acrogram for the word "focus" that I really like: Follow One Course Until Successful. Focusing your team on a mission statement or social justice issue is a powerful way to make an impact in your community. As

I've said many times already, audiences want the opportunity to attach themselves to a brand that shares their same beliefs.

While being polarizing can cause you to lose members or to alienate those who don't share the same values, the fact is this separation is entirely the point! Stranding for something can bring together a group of like-minded people who are all moving in the same direction. A community (or record label roster) united under one banner will attract more people and will have a greater impact than a label who lacks a clear identity.

Today's independent record labels are far more connected with their audiences than ever before. There's a strange customer/company chemistry that people actively seek out. People like to support other people. They like when a customer service interaction turns into a dialog about each person's favorite vinyl color, or when an Instagram DM about an upcoming release date turns into a chance for them to express their appreciation. Let's look for ways where we can create opportunities for connection like these ones. Show your community that there's a real person behind your label, someone they can chat with, share ideas with, and most importantly, someone who shares their values.

Quick Tip: *If you're comfortable (and if it makes sense), put your name in your social media bio. You can even include a note that encourages people to reach out to you by name!*

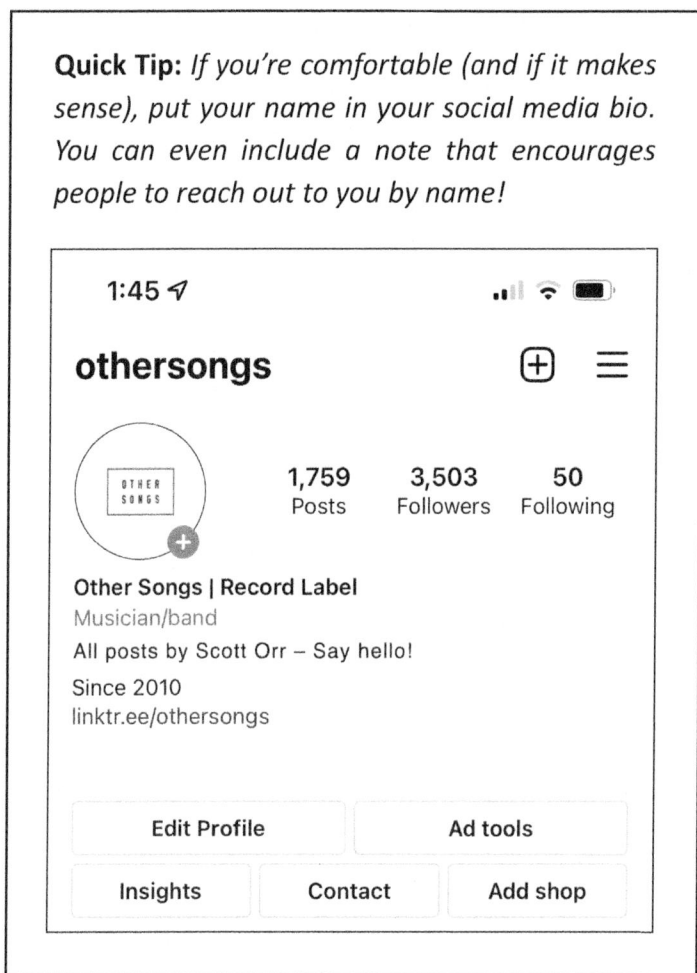

1:45 ✈

othersongs   ⊕ ≡

1,759   **3,503**   **50**
Posts   Followers   Following

Other Songs | Record Label
Musician/band
All posts by Scott Orr – Say hello!
Since 2010
linktr.ee/othersongs

Edit Profile		Ad tools
Insights	Contact	Add shop

Citrus City Records is a great example of a record label with an engaging personality. The Richmond, VA label is run by Manny Lemus who is an incredible advocate for independent artists and who exists as a platform for self-expression.

In 2020 he told Pitchfork, "A lot of our artists take on subject matters like race issues or biracial/queer identities in ethnic cultures. Personal identity and music go hand-in-hand." Visit **citruscityrecords.bandcamp.com** to check them out!

CHAPTER ELEVEN
MANAGING YOUR ARTISTS' CAREER EXPECTATIONS

How to ensure that you and your artists are on the same page.

A lot of artists are naive to how things work in the music business, and why shouldn't they be? You want them to focus on creating and honing their art. However, because of this naivete, it is your responsibility to help them understand what they can realistically expect to come from their relationship with your label.

I've worked with artists who have had completely unrealistic expectations on how many records they will sell, or how easy it will be to sell tickets to their shows. It is not our job to discourage them, but to help prepare them for a career trajectory that takes persistence and patience.

Here's how to properly manage your artists' expectations...

1. Keep Track of Your Efforts

Maintain a spreadsheet of all the tasks and promotional pitches you've done on behalf of the artist. This will eliminate any suspicion in the artist's mind that their label isn't doing enough to promote their release. A mediocre album campaign should not be the result of a lack of effort on the label's part.

2. Under-promise

Be overly realistic with your artists. Keep them grounded in the reality that most press pitches get ignored, most singles don't get playlisted, and most albums don't break even. Don't be discouraging, instead, manage their expectations and leave room for them to be pleasantly surprised when their release *is* successful.

3. Over-deliver

While tempering your artists' expectations, you should also aim to exceed their newly lowered expectations. Being overly generous and putting in the extra effort can help you find ways to over-deliver to your artists. Successfully tempering your artists' expectations provides you with the headroom to impress.

You can effectively and compassionately manage your artists' expectations by bringing them along for the ride, showing them who you are pitching their music to, what opportunities you are pursuing, and comparing their numbers with previous campaigns. You can also help temper their presuppositions by under-promising what you can do for them, while over-delivering in areas you are extra skilled.

Quick Tip: *Before releasing their single or album, ask the artist what their idea of "success" looks like. If it is radio play, put most of your attention into college radio. If their idea of a successful release is getting placed on a prominent Spotify playlist, then put your focus on pitching to curators and Spotify's editorial team. Let the artist define the target that you should be aiming at.*

Make a list of three things you can do to help temper your artists' expectations. Then make a list of three ways you can maybe *exceed* their expectations.

CHAPTER TWELVE
THE 12-MONTH PROMOTIONAL STRATEGY

A simplified way to tackle an entire year of promotion in one day.

Planning a year's worth of promotions for your record label can be extremely daunting and such a task makes you see all forest and no trees. The problem most record labels face is trying to stay consistently connected with their audience in an effective and creative way. The daily demand of social media is time-consuming; YouTube and blogs require weekly content and email lists are challenging to nurture.

Furthermore, too many of us are reactive instead of proactive. When we see one of our peers engaging in a sale or launching a YouTube channel, we feel pressured to follow suit or run the risk of missing out on potential success.

I've come up with a simple strategy to help you consolidate your efforts and simplify your record label's promotions for an entire year.

The solution is to assign a promotional "theme" to each month of the year. Monthly themes can be a new album campaign, a focus on a social justice issue, highlighting a specific artist, or a seasonal sale. With this approach, you can literally plan out the next 12 months in a single day. This gives you (and your team) a promotional perimeter that will help guide your decision making.

Stick to a timeline that you can maintain in a healthy manner. A monthly theme is ideal for most record labels that are one-person operations. Quarterly themes can be even easier, but perhaps less effective. If you are a larger indie label, with multiple team members, maybe weekly themes are something that could be even more effective.

Maintaining a consistent promotional presence week after week, month after month, is an intimidating task. Breaking down the responsibilities into 12 manageable themes will ease this process and help reduce unnecessary stress.

Here are some of the benefits of an approach like this...

1. Lightening the Promotional Load

Sometimes the hardest part of maintaining a social media presence is coming up with ideas about what you should post. Promoting is easy when you have something significant to promote. Staying consistent becomes hard when you're not in the middle of an album cycle, or during a slow season. There's a guilt that comes with failing to populate your channels or a FOMO (fear of missing out) from not actively contributing to the conversation.

Having a predetermined topic takes away the unknown and eliminates the need to come up with something exciting on the fly.

For example, if December is generally a slow month for your label, commit the entire month to talking about a cause or charity that is important to you and your audience. Each week share a story with your audience that pertains to the month's message or run a fundraiser for the entire month and share its progress with your supporters.

2. Being Proactive Instead of Reactive

In addition to taking away the stress of not knowing what to share on social media, this strategy also helps you become more intentional on a regular basis, as opposed to acting spontaneous and disorganized. I've had my own experiences of FOMO like when I noticed a record label running a Black Friday sale on their website. I quickly threw together some graphics, a coupon code, and launched my own sale as fast as possible. This isn't a great way to run any business. You should be proactive instead of reactive, creative instead of competitive.

3. Staying on Message

Consistency enhances communication. We are most effective when we stay focused on one message at a time. Implementing a year-long strategy will create intentional bumpers to help you and your team stay on message. There will always be room for spontaneity and unexpected announcements, but your overall message will remain clear to your audience. "Success is the natural consequence of consistently applying the basic fundamentals" says entrepreneur, Jim Rohn. You will not bore your audience; you will not annoy them. They will subconsciously appreciate your consistency far more than having to process a litany of competing messages. Repetition isn't necessarily a bad thing.

This strategy is meant to help you stay organized and to reduce the pressure that comes with maintaining an active online presence. It should still allow for spontaneity and surprise promotions. Your goal with a 12-month promotional campaign is to get better at promoting records and finding new listeners and to be more intentional with how you operate as a record label.

This is an internal process that is meant to help motivate and organize you and your team. This strategy can be something that guides you and keeps you on message throughout the year. It is not necessary to let your audience know about your themes if it doesn't make sense to do so.

Quick Tip: *Here's a list of potential themes that may help give you some ideas for your record label's own monthly themes:*

- Fan appreciation month
- Social justice issue
- Specific artist on your label
- Other record labels in your genre or region
- Back-catalog month
- An album's special anniversary (10-year, 1-year)
- Your label's birthday month
- Seasonal sales (Christmas, Summer, Black Friday)
- Promote a new release
- Celebrate your local community/music scene
- Celebrate your genre or history of your music
- Celebrate a specific format with a sale (50% off vinyl)
- Celebrate indie record stores
- Celebrate a specific instrument for a month
- Celebrate a marginalized group in your community/genre
- A month dedicated to behind-the-scenes label operations
- Dedicate a month sharing what you've learned in the music business
- Dedicate a month to launching a new product (subscription, merch, Patreon, YouTube channel)
- Dedicate a month to promoting your merch/apparel
- Celebrate an ideology for the month (empathy, community, generosity, etc.)
- Highlight your year in review (stats, accomplishments, releases, etc.)

Go to http://geni.us/12-month-calendar to download a FREE printable promotional calendar that you can use for your record label!

PART THREE
ARTIST AND RELEASE MARKETING

CHAPTER THIRTEEN
PLANNING AN EFFECTIVE ALBUM ROLLOUT
Building a strategic, slow-drip release plan.

The primary purpose of an "album rollout" is to build anticipation while slowly dripping singles and album details. While a "campaign" focuses more on the promotional responsibilities of a new release, a rollout is more about the schedule and timeline of what will be released and in what order.

Here are the three levers record labels can pull to ensure an effective album rollout...

1. Ideal Lead Times

The lead time is the period between when the release has been mastered to when you schedule your release day. A few years ago, I was interviewing the marketing director of Sub Pop and they told me that they try to give their new releases a 22-week buffer. Today, vinyl production can take up to 10-12 months, so it is quite possible that labels are using a lead time upwards of 52 weeks! Ultimately, you can create whatever timeline works for your artist and your record label, and your timeline can be less severe if you're releasing only on digital.

With that being said, here are the lead times I like to recommend:
- Album: 8-16 weeks
- EP: 6-8 weeks
- Single: 4-6 weeks

This depends entirely on how complicated your manufacturing plans are and how ambitious your promotional goals are. It also depends on the preferred timeline of your publicist, as well as your artist.

2. **Compartmentalizing Your Strategies**

It helps to put your strategies and responsibilities into multiple compartments. This will give you a bird's eye view of how your release campaign is shaping up. It will also help you highlight where your campaign is weak and what marketing categories need improvement.

Categories can include:
- Playlisting/Streaming
- Manufacturing
- Radio
- Blogs/Press

- Influencers
- Email Marketing
- In-Person Events

3. Drip Releasing Content

I don't like to refer to singles or merchandise as "content" because it devalues the hard work and creativity of the artists. However, for the purpose of this chapter, it helps to think of our promotional assets as content.

Promotional assets include pre-release singles, tour dates, album title, artwork, new press photos, and other unreleased material that can help build anticipation for your new release.

Be strategic and intentional with how you release these pieces. After you've taken inventory, schedule a "slow drip" of exciting content and ensure you've picked the right platform to deliver this content to your fans.

The album rollout is where we implement our promotional strategies prior to release day. Not only will a successful rollout build anticipation, but it should also provide you with a framework that guides you to release day. Choose a release day that allows for a generous lead up and organize your promo initiatives into compartments to help provide clarity on what areas need most attention. Once you've taken stock of all your promotional plans and assets, begin to release lead-up singles, album details, and new merchandise in a strategic, scheduled manner.

Keep in mind that no two rollouts will ever be the same. Be flexible and open to pivot if something didn't go as planned, or if you encounter unexpected opportunities.

> **Quick Tip:** *The intensity of your release rollout should increase the closer you get to release day. Information and content released early in the rollout should tease the audience and create excitement, whereas promotional initiatives later in the rollout should be more substantial and impactful.*

To help you map out your new release's rollout, you can download a free copy of my Release Roadmap at **otherrecordlabels.com/roadmap.**

CHAPTER FOURTEEN
PICKING A RELEASE DATE
Choosing the most optimal day to release your project.

One of the first steps of a new release campaign is to pick a release day. This is the official day the single, album, or EP will be released to the public on all streaming platforms and/or in stores.

A successful release campaign starts with a strategically chosen release day. This date must be far enough into the future to allow your team to fully prepare. Preparations can include creating social media content, music videos, manufacturing records, and planning a tour. Your release plan must also allow for promotional efforts to happen after release day.

Here are a few things to consider when picking a release date...

1. Considering the Margin

Allow one to two months before and after your release date to properly promote your record. This provides promotional opportunities prior to the release, plus it allows you to create a supportive post-release plan. For example, if you pick a release date in March, you have January and February as a lead-up, and April to May for post-release promotions. However, a release day in early December would allow for a generous pre-release season (Sept-Nov) but your post-release plans may be ruined by the busy holiday season. For this reason, consider a release strategy that gives you time before and after release day to accomplish all you have planned for this new release.

2. Considering the Season

Ensure your new release doesn't come out on or around national and regional holidays. Look at the calendar and ensure that you avoid any major events that could take attention away from your special day. Some things are of course unavoidable, just ensure that you research local, regional, national, and even international calendars to find a date that is least occupied. It is also wise to look at non-holiday events that could distract from your release's special day (e.g., elections, festivals, releases by major artists).

3. Considering the Timing

Make sure you check your release date with other key players on your team. Ensure that the timing works for your band or artist. Do they have a wedding to attend at that time? A work trip, or a previous commitment? Also, make sure to keep your release far enough away from other releases on your label to not cannibalize their campaigns.

A strategically chosen release day – with 4-6 months lead time –will help give your new release its best chance for success. A generous lead time creates a buffer for the unexpected and will allow time for more promotional initiatives to be accomplished. Remember to choose a release day that allows a margin before and after release day, this means a release day that is not too close to the end of a season or too soon after a major holiday event.

Having said that, there is something to be said about releasing something in a previously ill-advised season. It may offer your release an opportunity to shine. For example, December is generally avoided for new releases, but the end-of-year radio silence also makes it easier to cut through the noise. Keep in mind, it may not work, and the release may be ignored, you may want to try this strategy out with a live album or a lower priority release.

Choose a release date that works well for your artists, your team, and for your audience. Ensure your release day allows enough time to do everything you hoped to do for this release.

> **Quick Tip:** *Keep your digital distributor in the loop long before your scheduled release day. Check with your rep first to ensure that you can make the release day in time, and if there's anything else you need to be aware of.*

Visit **otherrecordlabels.com/releaseday** for more helpful tips on planning your upcoming release!

CHAPTER FIFTEEN
LEVERAGING THE POWER OF LEAD TIME
Providing your releases the time they need to succeed.

The strategic use of lead time is key to the success of a new release. Lead time is the amount of time from the start of an album to its release date. More specifically, in marketing for a new release, I consider lead time to be the time between when the masters are complete, and when the album (or single) is released to the public.

A lot of independent artists finish recording on a Saturday, master on a Sunday, and release on a Monday. There is something beautiful about the spontaneity of home-recording, and the ease of distribution that today's technology provides. However, a negative byproduct of this immediacy is the failure of artists to give their audience the joy of anticipation. Additionally, giving time for the press and playlist curators will create more chances for your record to succeed.

Here's how to build lead time into your upcoming album campaign...

1. Creating a Workback Schedule

Here's how a workback schedule works: Let's

say you're hosting a birthday party on Saturday, March 6 at 8 pm. That means that you need to go pick up the cake at 5 pm before the guests arrive and before the cake store closes. To pick up the cake on Saturday afternoon, you will have needed to order the cake a few days prior. Plus, you will need to invite your guests a week or two before the night to make sure they're free to attend. If your party has a theme or a special gift for the guest of honor, you will want to make sure you start planning for that a month or more in advance.

This is how a workback schedule helps you achieve a successful album release (or birthday party). Once you've picked a release date for your album or single, begin by working backward from that date. Identify ahead of time, any deliverables that need to be acquired for your release day to be a success.

2. Starting the Campaign Early

The recording phase is a great time to have conversations with the artists about their goals for this release, their tour plans, and what ideas they have for album art.

3. Delaying Your Release Date Announcement

If you are patient enough, it is best if you wait until your test pressings are in hand before you set an official release date. Or if you are only releasing digitally, wait until the album is mastered. Some of you may find that hard to believe – and hard to accomplish – but you must allow for anything (or everything) to go wrong.

The artist can be indecisive about the album artwork, the mix engineer could be backed up with other projects, or the test pressings might have errors in them that will significantly delay the vinyl pressing. To compensate for some of these potential hold-ups, you and the artist should wait as far into the process as possible to announce your release date.

This doesn't mean you can't internally pick a release date much earlier; I encourage that. But announcing your release date too early lets the cat out of the bag and makes it harder for you to change the date if something comes up that will delay the process. Changing a release date after it is announced will make you and the artist look disorganized at best, or worse, unprofessional.

You can't be too early when it comes to planning an album release. Only bad things come from being rushed. Remember this great quote from Benjamin Franklin, "Failing to plan is planning to fail!" The length of your lead time is ultimately up to you. Set yourself a generous deadline that budgets extra time, and that you're capable of beating.

Quick Tip: *Having sufficient lead time is something I recommended most of the time. However, there is something special about a surprise album release. Artists of all sizes and popularity levels still surprise-drop records by announcing the album's existence the day of or the day before its release. This technique uses the element of surprise as the main source of promotion. If a traditional album campaign is a jet taking off from taxiing, then a surprise album release is a rocket leaving the earth in a few seconds. But be warned, once an album (and all its potential singles) has been released out into the world, its mystery can't be reclaimed. Make sure you think twice about a surprise release, consider giving one or two singles their own day in the sun.*

Our Record Label Toolkit contains a sample Release Roadmap as well as a copy of my Workback Schedule. You can download them for free at **otherrecordlabels.com/toolkit**

CHAPTER SIXTEEN
WRITING AN ARTIST BIO
Crafting an artist and release bio to help promote your new release.

An artist biography is a short description of the artist, their inspirations, and sonic qualities. The length of an artist bio can vary. However, it is probably best to keep it brief. At the very least, have a shortened version of the bio available with the option for the recipient to read more if they care to.

An artist (or release) bio is a valuable tool that you'll call upon many times during a release campaign. In addition to including it in your press pitch to members of the media, you'll also want to update your various web properties (Spotify, record label website, artist website, Instagram) with your new bio.

I recently interviewed the writer/journalist Sammy Maine about the art of writing a creative artist biography, and I want to highlight some of the incredibly helpful insights that came from our conversation.

Here are some helpful takeaways from that interview...

1. Artist Bio vs. Release Bio

In addition to writing an artist biography, it is

also advantageous to write a short description of the new release. Your new release one-sheet should include both biographies. An artist bio focuses more on the long-term career and artistic qualities of your artist, whereas a release bio highlights the message, inspiration, and sonics of the artist's new release.

2. Descriptive Email Subjects

One of those most clever tips that came out of my interview with Sammy was her idea to use the subject line of your pitch email to describe the new release. For example, "Debut EP from Chicago-based punk band." Members of the music media receive hundreds of press pitches each week, and an inviting subject line may increase the chances of your email getting opened.

3. A Conversation with The Artist

Another helpful tip from my interview with Sammy is to record you and your artist having an informal conversation about their upcoming project (tour or new release). Record the conversation on a voice recorder app, listen back to the conversation (or transcribe) and pull-out one-liners and meaningful reflections from the artist's own words to use in your album/artist bio.

An artist bio doesn't need to be complicated. It should clearly communicate what makes the artist special and unique. Additionally, a release bio can cover topics such as production elements, key personnel, accolades, and the key themes found in the lyrics.

Quick Tip: *Avoid cliches, name-dropping, typos, self-deprecation, or arrogant wording. Be authentic and humble. Ensure that the bio clearly communicates who your artist is and what their new release is trying to accomplish.*

You can grab a copy of a free artist bio template in our Record Label Toolkit: **otherrecordlabels.com/toolkit**. Also, you can get in touch with Sammy Maine if you need help crafting your bio, visit **otherrecordlabels.com/directory** to connect!

CHAPTER SEVENTEEN
THE ALBUM CAMPAIGN PRE-MORTEM
Anticipating and strategizing the outcomes for your release campaigns.

In this book, I try to highlight a multitude of things you can do to contribute to the success of your new releases, and your record label. But sometimes efforts and good intentions aren't enough, and you may want to prepare for the worst.

A novel way to be ultra-prepared is something I call, "the album campaign pre-mortem." Instead of waiting until after release day to conduct a post-mortem (an internal evaluation process that generally takes place after a project has ended with the goal of improving future projects), record labels should be proactive and anticipate what could go wrong.

A pre-mortem imagines that a project or initiative has failed. This exercise works backwards to determine what could potentially lead to the failure of the project, and how your team may be able to create contingency plans or avoid failure altogether.

Establish your expectations prior to release day - set goals, action steps, and assign responsibilities to ensure everyone is doing their part. Identify what areas of the existing release plan are weakest and discuss how you can make improvements before it's too late. Establishing your goals and expectations will give you something to aim for and help bring clarity to everyone involved in the release campaign. Look for areas that are weak or that lack strategy and try to reinforce these efforts before the campaign gets underway. Finally, add a level of insurance to the release by jotting down some backup ideas in the event that your initial goals aren't met.

Here are a few ways you can be proactive to tackle problems with your release campaign before they happen!

1. Establishing Expectations

Take a moment to outline the goals and expectations of the artist and the label. What would need to happen for this campaign to be a success? What are some of the "bare-minimum" expectations you have for this release? What might be some lofty goals that would surprise the team? Declaring each party's expectations will not only help you achieve your goals, but it can also help mitigate any potential conflicts between you and your artists.

Book a meeting with the artist, band members, managers, and record label staff. Ask everyone to bring their own list of expectations. The chart below is an example of how each person can organize and communicate their expectations for the upcoming release campaign.

Must Haves	Nice to Haves	Lofty Goals
EXAMPLE: Physical records in-house on release day	EXAMPLE: Article/review on a prominent music site	EXAMPLE: Placement on an official Spotify playlist

2. Identifying Weak Areas

It is helpful to be honest with yourself by pin-pointing any areas of weakness in your release plan. Oftentimes, our weaknesses are our blind spots, and are therefore hard to identify. It may not be possible to truly know what your label's weaknesses are. Therefore, it is essential that you try to estimate where your release plan might fall short, to be more prepared.

Evaluate your label's past album campaigns to identify what elements were missing. Use your previous post-mortems to inform your future releases. If your artist has previously self-released music, ask them to help pinpoint what areas of their release went well and what initiatives fell flat.

A proper stress test won't be possible until it's

too late – when the campaign is in full swing – the best you can do is try to identify the weak spots in your own abilities.

3. Creating a Back-up Plan

Part of building a comprehensive release strategy is installing a back-up plan if some expectations aren't met. Creating a "Plan B" can be a great way to add depth and resilience to your release campaign.

You can even reuse the above spreadsheet that outlines your goals and expectations to also include an alternate plan in case your initial strategy isn't effective.

Example:

Must Haves	Nice to Haves	Lofty Goals
EXAMPLE: Physical records in-house on release day	EXAMPLE: Article/review on a prominent music site	EXAMPLE: Placement on an official Spotify playlist
BACK-UP: Order prints of the album artwork to sell until the records arrive	BACK-UP: Recruit your friend circle to share your new release on their Instagram stories all day	BACK-UP: Use Submit Hub to pitch a single to smaller, more accessible playlists

You may want to implement some of your back-up plans regardless of how the campaign is going. Either way, it is helpful to have more than one promotional strategy in place.

There's no need to be dramatic or make assumptions that are unfounded. The pre-mortem analysis is meant to identify threats and weaknesses via the hypothetical presumption of what could go wrong. At the end of the day, if everyone is clear about their expectations and responsibilities, you should feel confident in your plans.

Quick Tip: *The pre-mortem strategy is a novel concept that can help improve your preparedness. It can be a fun and helpful part of the process, but the unknown and the unpredictable will always interrupt the best laid plans. So don't put too much pressure on trying to predict the future.*

Listen to the series "Release Roadmaps" on the *Other Record Labels* podcast. In these interviews, I talk with record labels about their recent release rollouts. What went right and what areas they could have improved on.
Go to **otherrecordlabels.com/listen**

CHAPTER EIGHTEEN
HIRING A MUSIC PUBLICIST
Knowing when and how to hire a music publicist.

A music publicist is an individual (or an agency) that assists an artist (or record label) in creating a marketing campaign for their new release. Publicists can work for independent artists directly, through their management team, or they can be hired separately by the record label. A music publicist can be hired for a specific single campaign or a full album campaign. In some cases, more established artists will even opt to have a publicist on retainer on an ongoing basis.

The work of a music publicist can vary, but for the most part they are meant to convince members of the press to feature an album (or single). This may include promoting the new release to bloggers, magazines, music sites, curators, journalists, newspapers, playlisters, radio stations, and other notable influencers. Some publicists will assist the record label in creating a strategic album campaign that spans over a specific period.

While music publicists can be incredibly effective in promoting a record, a lot of labels can't afford their services, and choose to manage their release campaigns internally. The purpose of this book is to help you run successful album campaigns on your own. However, sometimes a successful campaign requires outsourcing and partnering with other skilled individuals.

Here are some things you should know about hiring a music publicist...

1. The Cost

The cost of a good publicist can vary from $500 to $5000 per campaign. A reputable agency - with a proven track record and a capable team - can charge upwards of $10,000 for an album campaign. While I'm sure there are some special exceptions, publicists who charge $500 or less for an album campaign may produce mixed results. A competent publicist is someone who has relevant contacts in the media, is organized, and who is respected in the industry.

2. Finding a Publicist

The best way to find a music publicist that will work well for your record label is to find out who your peers have previously hired. Research which publicists or agencies were behind album campaigns that you've admired in the past. Furthermore, find a publicist who has worked for artists and labels that are like yours. This is a great place to start as it will help guide you in finding an individual who knows your audience, and who has contacts in the genres you represent.

3. Preparing a Timeline

Long lead times are critical for successful album campaigns. This is a drum you will hear me pound a lot. When working with a music publicist, make sure you give them a lot of advanced time to work their magic. Any good publicist will need to be booked several months in advance (stay clear of anyone who will take your money a few days before release day). For example, if you have a new release scheduled for June, you should start booking your publicist in January!

Ensure that you manage your expectations before you hire a publicist. Even the best publicist can't make people like something. Music is subjective and there's a lot of luck and timing that goes into making a successful release.

It is best to think of a music publicist as a partner or a temporary employee of your label. Empower them to handle the task of pitching the album so you can free yourself to focus on another part of the release campaign like manufacturing, distribution, or licensing.

Quick Tip: *Before you start shopping around for a music publicist, make a list of things you expect the publicist to do for you. Clearly stating your expectations before you sign any agreements will provide both parties with key result areas to aim for.*

Listen to my interview with Jamie Coletta, a talented music publicist who runs the incredible PR agency, No Earbuds: **otherrecordlabels.com/listen**

CHAPTER NINETEEN
PITCHING MUSIC TO PRESS PUBLICATIONS

Submitting your upcoming release to blogs, curators, influencers, and journalists.

Whether you're hiring a publicist or handling your PR in-house, it is important to know how to effectively (and respectfully) pitch your music to the press.

Most record labels spend years building a genuine list of press contacts that they pitch to on a regular basis. Regardless of where you're at in your label's timeline, maintain a spreadsheet of curators, press outlets, journalists, DJs, influencers, and industry contacts. These contacts are more than just email addresses; they should be real people who you interact with regularly. Nurture your contacts in an authentic and genuine way by supporting their work and communicating with them regularly, not just when you need something from them.

Here are a few things that will help you when pitching to the press...

1. Artist and Album Bios

I have seen some incredibly wordy pitches. Press pages with lengthy bios come off as arrogant and presumptuous. Keep in mind that a lot of writers and publications receive over a hundred pitches from artists each day. A pitch containing a sea of words is highly unlikely to be read. A more effective approach is to provide a short paragraph (2-3 sentences) that tells the story of why this release is special and why it will matter to a listener. Stick to point form details and if the publication likes what they hear, they will reach out to you for a more exhaustive artist biography.

You should also use the subject line of your pitch email as a "mini-bio" for your album (e.g., An emotive, ambient folk record. For fans of Bon Iver, Helado Negro). The subject line of emails is a valuable piece of real estate and what you write could determine whether a writer/blogger/curator will open it. Use this space to be concise and clear with what type of release is being pitched.

2. Press One-Sheets

Putting a simple one-sheet together is quite easy to do and can be helpful for writers and curators to learn more about the release. In its simplest form, you can use a document that includes things like album cover, artist bio, release date, production credits, press photo, photographer credit, UPC code, track list, pre-release singles, artist social media links, label contacts, and a short album description.

There is no need to reinvent the wheel for every new release. Duplicate your template and repopulate the fields for your newest release. Recently, I've been using a singular, password-protected web page within Squarespace that I've designed to be my one-sheet template. This template can be easily re-used for subsequent releases.

See example: (over)

Illitry
Dalinean Horses

Bio

Hamilton's Illitry (aka Troy Witherow) has been steadily making a name for himself releasing singles and playing some pretty high-profile shows with his live band in Steeltown. And today, we're very excited to present the premiere of his debut EP The Sunset:

The four-track release starts off fiercely with some very in-your-face melancholy electronic pop, with the riveting opening song "Fall". The interplay between Witherow's soaring soft vocals and his sleek synths is simply magical, and it's our favourite song from him to date! Those incredible vocals resurface in "Easy Way Out", which features remarkable Bon Iver-esque harmonies over a heavy beat that you wouldn't expect. The record was produced by Michael Kiere.

Listen

SoundCloud Private Link

Bandcamp Private Link

October 2, 2020

Track Listing

1. Roman Walls
2. Copper Sun
3. Aphrodite
4. Like Everyone Else
5. Water Sounds
6. Hedge My Bets
7. Where You Go
8. Ghost
9. Polish Rose
10. KEF

Running Time
21 min

Label
Your Label Name

SKU/Catalog ID
192914711575 / OSM059

Genre
Electronic

Location
City, State, Country

Artist Social Links
Instagram: @illitry
Twitter: @illitry
Website: illitry.com

Contact
Scott Orr
scott@othersongsmusic.com
905.555.5555
www.othersongsmusic.com
youtube.com/othersongs
instagram.com/othersongs
twitter.com/othersongs

Photo Credit: Photographer's Name

Artist Press Page

3. An Example of a Press Pitch Outline

When pitching a new release to the press, and in the absence of a comprehensive press one-sheet, you should write something like the following in the body of your pitch email...

Artist: Artist
Album: Album Title
Release Date: Date
Credits: Production, guest artists, mixed by, etc.
Label: Your Label name
Format: Digital/Cassette/Vinyl (UPC: #)

Release Online-Liner: *One or two interesting sentences to describe the new release. Eg. An electro-acoustic debut from Carolina band, The Jones. Combining organic piano and percussion with brash synthesizers and drum machines.*

Tracklist:
1. Song
2. Song
3. Song
4. etc...

Pre Release Single #1: "Song" (Date)
Pre Release Single #2: "Song" (Date)
Pre Release Single #3: "Song" (Date)

Streaming Private Link: Easy private streaming link
Preorder: Bandcamp Preorder Link or Spotify Pre-save
Instagram: Link to artist Instagram or popular social channel (optional)

Bio: A one or two-paragraph artist bio.

Label (or Publicist) Contact Details: Name, Email, Phone

You must work towards building long-term relationships with your press contacts - not throwing press releases at the wall to "see what sticks." Mass emails will get you ignored and don't do your artist and their art any justice.

Hardworking record labels know that genuine relationships with the press takes time. It may take a few pitches, over a couple of years, for writers and blogs to get to know you. Keep track of your interactions with the writers who support your label's releases and make your correspondence as personal as possible. Use a spreadsheet to keep track of your contacts, who they write for, and what previous releases they've written about. These steps will help you develop lasting relationships with writers, bloggers, and curators.

Lastly, if a publication writes about your release, or a curator includes a song on their playlist, or a DJ plays your track, reach out and say "thanks." The simple act of gratitude will go a long way.

Quick Tip: *Generally speaking, singles should be sent to the press 2-4 weeks before they are released. Whereas albums need closer to 2-4 months of lead-time.*

Check out our online course, *Record Label Marketing Strategies* that contains a standalone module on how to create a Press One-Sheet that also includes templates in Word, Photoshop, and PDF.
Visit: **otherrecordlabels.com/courses**

CHAPTER TWENTY
MANAGING YOUR CONTENT ASSETS

Creating a unified strategy for your promotional pieces.

There's more than just the music itself that you can utilize to help promote a new release. New album details, photos, behind-the-scenes content, and alternate mixes can all be utilized throughout the album rollout, prior to release day and after.

To be most effective with this content, it is essential that you catalog all your promotional assets in one central location, prior to launching the album campaign.

Organizing these promo pieces will help you and your artist stay organized, intentional, and efficient with promoting the new release.

Here are a few ways you can manage your content assets...

1. Creating a Centralized Location

Use a cloud-based file management system (Dropbox, Google Drive) to house all of your promo assets and provide access to your team, the artist's team, your publicist, and possibly members of the press.

Here are a few things that can be included:
- early song demos
- behind-the-scenes videos/photos
- recording notes/production ideas
- video content
- music videos
- MP3 and WAV versions of the final album
- high resolution album artwork
- photoshoot photos
- press clippings
- photo mockups of the physical records
- press one-sheets
- album lyrics

2. Creating a Centralized Information Document

It is important that you keep track of all the specific details that pertain to your new release. I like to create a spreadsheet that houses all this information in one, centralized place (see example below). This way, I can share access to this document (I use Google Sheets) with the artist, manager, publicist, publishing administrator, and whoever else may need access to this.

Here are a few things that should be included in this document:
- Album title
- Release date
- Pre-release singles and release dates

- Track listing
- Songwriter/publishing information
- Link to press page
- Dropbox link to high-resolution press photo
- Photographer credits
- ISRCs for each track
- Dropbox link to album cover
- Download link to album (MP3s)
- ISWCs for each song
- Google Docs link with song lyrics
- Label catalog ID
- Album credits
- Album one-liner
- Artist bio

	A	B	C	D	E
Release Date:		6/22/2023		**Singles**	Date
Today's Date:		2/27/2022			
Days Until Release:		**480**			
Catalog ID					
Artist:					
Barcode:					
Title:					
IPI:					
Sounds Like:	(for fans of...)				
Lyrics:	(Google Doc Link)				
Photogragher Credit:					
Press Photo:	(Dropbox Link)				
Album Cover:	(Dropbox Link)				
Soundcloud Private Lin	(Soundcloud Link)				
Download Link:	(Dropbox Link)				
Tracklist	**Song Title**	**ISRC**	**ISWC**		

3. Creating a Content Release Schedule

Now that you've organized all your promotional content it is time to plan out how you're going to release everything. Look at the weeks leading up to your release and decide what promotional pieces you should utilize to generate anticipation and excitement. Similarly, save some content to schedule in the weeks (and even months) following the release. It is important to ensure that the artist and their team are aware of this content release schedule. Artists are often eager to release something as soon as it is ready, so make sure they know there's a plan in place.

Don't underestimate the promotional value of simple things like the album title, unreleased press photos, and behind-the-scenes content. Don't miss out on great opportunities to create anticipation for a new release and to extend the life of your promo campaign.

Quick Tip: *Start accumulating and organizing your content assets as early as possible. The songwriting and recording stage can produce a lot of great content that can be shared with fans. Treat this collection like a scrapbook or time capsule for the new release. Include photos from the recording sessions, album lyrics, initial artwork ideas, and unfinished mixes. All these things might come in handy later down the road when you're promoting the new release.*

Grab the free template of my "Album Information Document" on Google Sheets at **otherrecordlabels.com/record-label-resources**

CHAPTER TWENTY-ONE
THE VISUAL SIDE OF RELEASING MUSIC
Understanding the role of visuals in promoting music.

Recently I had an epiphany with how I discover music. Most of the music I discover I initially see on Instagram, through a tweet on Twitter, or perhaps even on YouTube. Even outside of social media, it is the album cover I see first when browsing for music on Spotify, AppleMusic, or in a record store!

Record labels need to find ways to leverage this reality to do a better job at convincing new listeners to check out their releases.

Most, if not all the new music I discover, I first see it before I hear it!

This should come as no surprise to us. We live in an incredibly visual world. Facebook knows this, that's why they bought Instagram and began slowly implementing videos, stories, and reels. Micro videos, photo sets, and infographics are everywhere online and are an important part of the music discovery process.

Here are a few ways you can attract listeners with their eyes...

1. Investing in Album Artwork

I am not suggesting that you need to have shocking or award-winning artwork. But what I am suggesting is that the album artwork shouldn't be an afterthought, it should be a significant part of the new release planning process and it should begin as early as the recording phase. Create a vision board (or Pinterest board) with the artist and include as many inspirational visuals as necessary. Look for artists you can hire, eye-catching fonts, and design styles that match the mood of the songs. Utilize bright colors or bold illustrations. Additionally, minimalism and the use of white space have all been proven to garner positive fan reactions.

While sometimes pricey, consider contracting a visual artist to create an overall aesthetic for a new album campaign. Hire them to create an album cover, album merchandise, web banners, and more. Do you follow any graphic artists or designers on Instagram that you admire? Reach out to them and ask how much they charge for an album cover.

2. Creating Realistic Product Images

Recently, I was speaking with Andrew Jervis from Bandcamp who expressed disappointment in how many artists fail to upload photos of their records, tapes, and merch to Bandcamp. A lot of artists simply upload a JPG of the album cover and fail to show real-life examples of their physical merch. If your records are still at the pressing plant, or you are selling print-on-demand t-shirts, simply use a digital mockup. These are real-life images that allow you to (using Photoshop) add your album cover or original design to create a photo of what the finished product might look like.

I have a few digital mockups for tapes and vinyl that you can download for free at otherrecordlabels.com.

The purpose of these real-life mockups is to help the fans visualize what the finished product will look like. If you do have the products in hand, take some in-action shots with them to share on social media or to include on your Bandcamp listing. There is a significantly higher perceived value when you show a simulated 3D image as opposed to a simple JPG of the album cover.

3. Sharing the Creative Process

There is a lot of visual content that record labels can harness from the artist's creative process.

This can include anything from handwritten lyrics, studio footage, concert photos, tour posters, or an intimate peek into the artist's creativity.
If the artist is comfortable with this level of transparency, encourage them to share behind-the-scenes photos, videos, or screenshots when promoting their new release.

A label's job is to share and promote the music, but this can be accomplished through more mediums than just sound. Visuals are driving today's online engagement, and they can provide you with an incredible opportunity to connect your artists with their audience.

Quick Tip: *Some record labels implement an aesthetic standard upon all their releases (e.g., Blue Note Records) if this is something you intend to do with your label, you will need to create a "style guide" that clearly outlines the visual requirements for each new release on your label. Some labels allow the artists to be the sole art director for their music, while other labels prefer more control over the visual presentation of the label's catalog.*

Check out my free tutorial on how to give your album campaign a visual brand: **otherrecordlabels.com/artwork**

CHAPTER TWENTY-TWO
DEVELOPING EFFECTIVE PLAYLISTING STRATEGIES

Understanding streaming and how to make a sustainable streaming strategy.

Playlists are ubiquitous, their popularity and potential profitability for indie labels has remained unwavering over the past few years. However, getting your music placde on one has become ever more evasive. Many questions remain for artists and record labels who pursue inclusion on these playlists. Who oversees curating them? Which ones generate the most plays? What moods and genres are most relevant to your record label?

Playlists provide a unique connection to passive music listeners. Active fans buy physical records, attend shows, and follow artists on social media. Whereas passive fans may not even know who they're listening to, but they still contribute to your label's success. A record label wants — needs — passive fans just as much as active fans.

Sometimes it is helpful to think of your label's streaming strategy as a funnel. At the top of your funnel (the widest part) are the passive listeners you garner from playlists. As the funnel narrows, the audience gets smaller, but their connection to the music strengthens. The narrowest point of your funnel will contain the smallest audience, but they will be the most highly engaged and supportive fans.

Using this visual, we can see how playlisting plays a pivotal role in bringing new listeners into your fan funnel in a frictionless, automated way.

PASSIVE FANS

STREAMING, PANDORA, RADIO

DOWNLOADS, LIVE MUSIC,
SOCIAL MEDIA

MERCH, VINYL,
PATREON

ACTIVE FANS

Here are the three categories of playlists that you should investigate...

1. Editorial Playlists

The most popular playlists are editorial playlists as they are official playlists created by the staff at the major digital service providers. In some cases (especially on Spotify), these playlists can have hundreds of thousands of listeners, which can translate into a sizable revenue stream. For this reason, they are the most prestigious and hardest to get placed on.

Spotify has the most robust online submission form through their Spotify for Artists platform. Make sure you sign up for this service (it's free) and follow the instructions to submit your new release for playlist consideration at least 4 weeks in advance.

AppleMusic also has a pitching process that in-volves a private Google doc, however you'll have to have a contact or a publicist who has access to this form.

2. Third-Party Playlists

A lot of popular brands will create playlists as a way to represent their company on Spotify and to project their brand's aesthetic. Examples of these include Starbucks, Aritzia, H&M, Sonos, etc.

Additionally, a lot of music blogs like NPR, Pitchfork, UPROXX also have their own ongoing playlists.

Unfortunately, most of these playlists aren't very approachable. You may want to try some outside-the-box attempts to pitch your music by searching for the playlist curators on LinkedIn or Twitter.

3. User-Generated Playlists

User-Generated Playlists (UGPs) are simply public playlists created by individual users. What makes these unique from third-party playlists is that they are often created as passion projects or as personal collections. These can be created by everyday Spotify users, your friends, or up-and-coming social media influencers. These are often more accepting of new artists, but they don't all have enough followers to earn the artist significant plays.

Playlisting should be a part of every record label's

marketing strategy. For some labels, streaming makes up a significant piece of the revenue pie, while for other labels, it is simply one small slice.

Diversifying your opportunities for success is critical. Identify the various types of playlists, the most popular moods, and genres, and create a plan to pitch to the most relevant playlists. Create special releases and regular social media content that reaches the wide audience of streaming fans. Whatever role streaming plays for your label, ensure that you do your part to serve the fans who enjoy playlists.

Quick Tip: *Be sure to fill in all the details when setting up your catalog on DSPs (digital service providers). This is a best practice that is too often overlooked. If a DSP has an artist platform, make sure you sign up and populate all the fields with up-to-date information (biography, latest photos, social media links). It is rumored that some of the algorithms of the major streaming platforms favor these best practices. Additionally, being organized creates brand consistency and improves the overall fan experience.*

One of the most up-to-date books on playlists and streaming is the book *Work Hard, Playlist Hard* by Mike Warner.
Learn more at
otherrecordlabels.com/streaming

CHAPTER TWENTY-THREE
THE POST-RELEASE STRATEGY
Keeping an album "alive" after release day.

If you've ever made a bonfire while camping you know that a lot of effort goes into getting the fire started. However, once you get a fire going, it will eventually die out, so you keep putting more logs on, and fanning the flames less they disappear.

It should go without saying that a new music campaign works the same way as a bonfire. After the initial flames of excitement, the release needs constant attention to stay alive.

Here are a few simple things your record label can do to ensure that you maximize the length of your release campaign...

1. Taking Inventory of Your Promotional Items.

Identify and take inventory of all your promotional assets. This can include things like music videos, remix stems, press photos, artist commentary, song lyrics, behind-the-scenes content, and more. Organize all your pieces into a centralized shared folder online (Dropbox, Google Drive) and share the link with your entire team (artists, manager, publicist, label). You may even want to create a spreadsheet to help you keep track of everything.

Example:

Item	Responsibility	Details	Release Date
Music Video	Band	Video for 2nd single	1 month after release day
Album Essay	Lead Singer	Essay about the meaning behind the album title	1 day after release day
B-Side	Label	Extra song from sessions	3 months after release

This exercise will show you what content you have at your disposal to help promote the new release. You won't know where your campaign is lacking until you first take stock of what promotional pieces you have. You may have to spend more time creating promotional content leading up to the release.

2. Making a Schedule

Once you have all your promotional items organized and identified, it's time to schedule a release date for each piece. For example, you may want to release a single two months prior to the album release, followed by the official album announcement (album cover release, album title announcement, pre-ordering goes live, etc.) a few days later.

You should have a plan for every piece of promotional content. More importantly, ensure that everyone is aware of what is permitted to be released, and when. Make sure your whole team (and the artist's team) is aware of this "slow drip of content" promotional strategy.

In fact, I try to adhere to this (loose) promotional schedule when it comes to how often I'm promoting a new release:

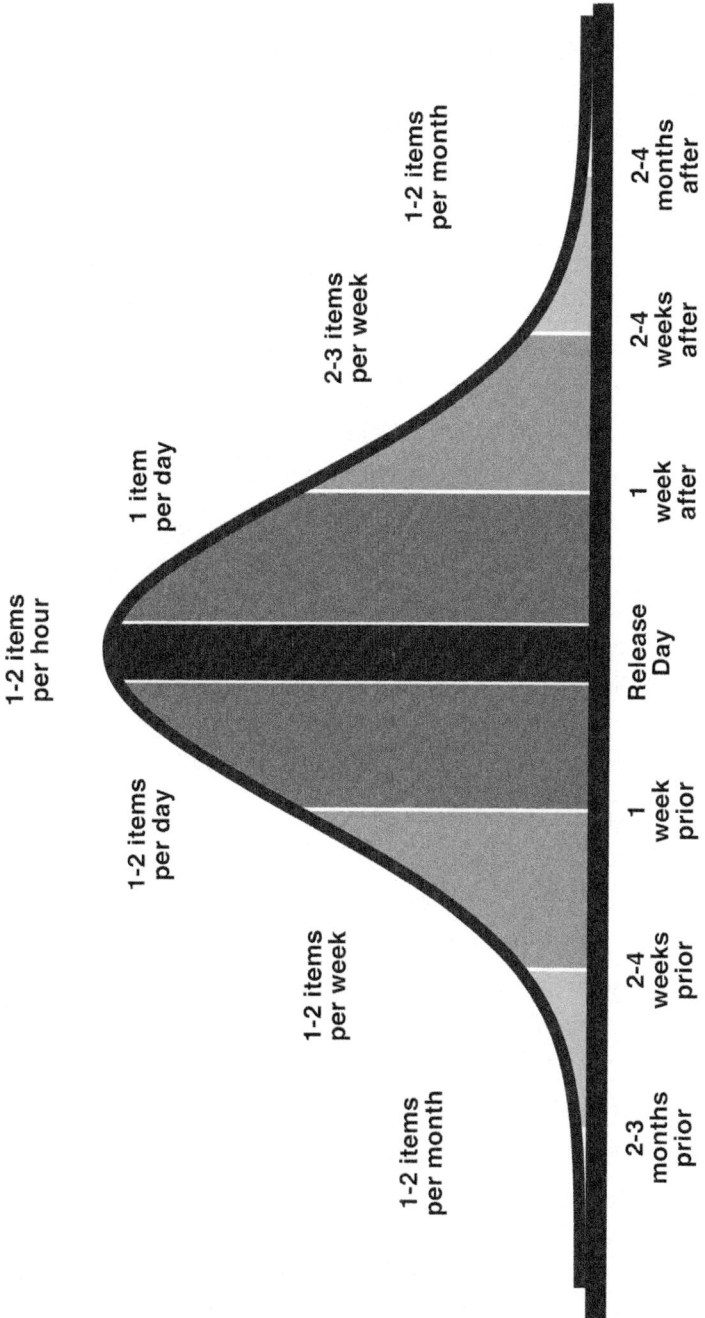

1-2 items per hour

1 item per day

1-2 items per day

2-3 items per week

1-2 items per week

1-2 items per month

1-2 items per month

2-3 months prior

2-4 weeks prior

1 week prior

Release Day

1 week after

2-4 weeks after

2-4 months after

3. Continuing Creativity

Record labels should encourage and empower the artists they work with to continue to be creative. If the artist is comfortable with being creatively productive, find ways to support them and to help them achieve their highest level of creativity.

There's also a lot that the record label can continue to do long after release day. You could manufacture and re-release on a new format (cassette, CD), press a new vinyl color variant, or drop a new line of merch.

My point is that creativity should continue throughout the entire album campaign, and beyond. Creativity shouldn't end when the music is mastered.

The traditional album cycle is becoming less relevant today as audiences expect to hear from the artists far more frequently.

Marketing doesn't end on release day. Music publicist Jamie Colletta often says that release day is *day one* of an entirely new release campaign. As you can see in the previous illustration, there is just as much content needed for the post-release campaign as the pre-release. This is the strategy I hope you're able to implement with your record label. Create a post-release marketing plan in the same way you developed your pre-release campaign.

Take inventory of your promotional assets and create a schedule with how you "slow drip" each piece of content. With the same effort it takes to build a fire, is how you should work to keep the fire burning.

Quick Tip: *Develop two official marketing campaigns for each release. One that starts a few months before release day, and a second campaign that officially starts the day after release day.*

I've made a special page on OtherRecordLabels.com to help you build your post-release plan.
Visit **otherrecordlabels.com/postrelease**

CHAPTER TWENTY-FOUR
UTILIZING VIDEO TO PROMOTE YOUR RELEASES
Using video content to help promote your artists and releases.

As an elder millennial with a face for podcasting, I've always been reluctant when it comes to creating video content. But the truth is, video is imperative in this day and age. It provides fans with an intimate peek behind the curtain and record labels can utilize video content such as in-studio footage, music videos, artist vlogs, and live streaming concerts. Luckily, technology has evolved where the tools for making quality video content have become more accessible and more affordable.

It is essential that you build a sustainable video strategy, one that falls within your capabilities, and that displays your label's unique personality.

Here are three types of video content record labels should be utilizing...

1. Behind-the-Scenes Content

I am often surprised at how few labels take time to share unfiltered videos of their label operations. There's no need to be self-conscious or worried that your processes aren't entertaining enough. So few record labels share in the process of packing orders, making music videos, or manufacturing merchandise and this can give fans a glimpse into how a record label works. You can do this by simply sharing short clips on Tik-Tok or Instagram Reels, or by creating more fully fleshed out weekly vlogs on YouTube.

2. Music Videos

In the late 1980s, a music video was as essential as the song itself. MTV was one of the fastest ways for a major label to turn their latest signing into a star. Today, even as music video platforms have come and gone, the value of a well-directed music video has remained. The good thing today is that you can create high-quality music videos on a fraction of the budget that labels paid in the 80s.

The purpose of a music video is twofold: 1) it is designed to reach music fans who are more visually stimulated. Music discovery happens differently for everybody, and music videos are cherished by fans who appreciate the visual interpretation of a song, and 2) music videos act as another promotional touch-point for fans. Some listeners may have forgotten to check out your new release, and a music video provides them a fresh reminder.

Some independent labels have been fortunate to work with high-caliber directors and filmmakers to shoot award-winning videos. At the same time, other labels have had equal success by creating low-budget videos that showcase the artist's personality and aesthetic.

It is also worthwhile to investigate what arts and music grants are available that can help you fund a music video for your artist. This is completely dependent on what programs your country or state offers the arts community.

3. Live Streaming

Streaming live music has been a technology that has been slow to evolve over the past decade. This is partly due to limited technology, in addition to fan resistance. Back in 2015, Facebook launched a live streaming feature that was only available to celebrities. At the same time, Twitter-owned Periscope was offering a livestream platform for anyone to utilize. Today, anyone can easily live stream in HD, directly from their phone, using already-adopted platforms like YouTube, Instagram, Twitch, and Facebook. Not only that, but the public's adoption of live streaming was expedited rapidly by the COVID-19 global pandemic, meaning fans (and your grandparents) are more accepting and equipped to participate in an online performance.

Using video as a promotional tool is practically a must-have for today's audiences. While demand for video is high, it doesn't mean that it must be demanding on you and your team. Develop a video strategy that you can maintain on an ongoing basis. Team up with individuals who are gifted in creating video content for TikTok or YouTube. At the same time, keep it simple, give fans a peek behind the curtain by sharing behind-the-scenes videos of your day-to-day label operations, or your artist's creative process.

> **Quick Tip:** *Don't overspend on video equipment for your record label, a modern smartphone should suffice for video quality. It is better to invest in individuals such as independent filmmakers, directors, and video editors. Don't try to do it all on your own!*

Recently, Bandcamp launched an interesting platform for independent artists to stream their live performances to their fans, with the option to monetize the event.
Visit **bandcamp.com/about_live** to learn more.

CHAPTER TWENTY-FIVE
MAKING THE MOST OF YOUR CATALOG
Amortizing your artist's financial and creative contributions.

In economics there are fixed costs and variable costs. Fixed costs are expenses that stay the same regardless of how much a company produces, while variable costs are any expenses that change, and scale based on the company's output.

In music production, fixed costs are things like recording studio expenses, mastering, photography, and artwork. Those costs are "fixed" and don't increase regardless of how many records you sell. Examples of variable costs in the music industry would be things like mailing list software, Facebook ads, or manufactured media (CDs, vinyl).

It is our responsibility as record labels to ensure that we utilize these fixed expenses to the full extent. This is what it means to "get your money's worth!"

Here are a few ways you can make sure you are making the most out of your fixed costs...

1. Maximizing Your Audio

Artists spend months writing new music and just

as much time if not more, recording and mixing. There is no better way to honor their efforts than to make sure their hard work is fully availed.

For example, a label can release an instrumental version of an album as a bonus release or later in the album cycle. Stems (individual instrument tracks) from the recording sessions can be re-used for remixes or to license to other producers. Remember, the recordings are a fixed cost, the expense of utilizing them to the full extent should be minimal.

2. Maximizing Your Artwork

If you have a respectful agreement in place with your visual artist, your team should be looking for ways to maximize your investment into the artwork. You can do this by printing band merchandise with the album artwork, creating similar album art for pre-release singles, and making use of the art to create promotional graphics for social media and tour posters.

Make sure the visual artist you've hired provides you with the layered art files and is fairly compensated for their initial work. Most work-for-hire agreements entitle you to utilize the artwork in other applications, however some artists may request a royalty if their work is further monetized.

3. Maximizing Your Release Rollout

Have you noticed how fans get excited when an artist they love announces a new album? Or when a band releases their upcoming tour schedule? These are all news items that garner attention for the artist and their latest release. Ensure that your team utilizes these pieces of information and make sure you have a plan for how you strategically release them. Announcing the album's track listing, first single, or premiering the album cover should all be made into an "event" that helps extend the promotional period of the album.

Here are a few examples of information that can be effective content:

- Release date
- Album artwork
- Music video release
- Tour itinerary
- Behind the scenes content
- Pre-release singles
- Album track listing
- Song lyrics
- Song descriptions/explanations

Maximizing each release is not only fiscally responsible but it serves as an act of respecting the art - ensuring that an artist's efforts are fully realized. One of the biggest problems artists and labels face in today's industry is how quickly albums "die" or lose their newsworthiness after release day. Spending time to ensure you discover all the ways you can promote a release, the songwriting, artwork, and recordings is critical to an album's success.

Quick Tip: *Ensure you acquire all the necessary promotional elements ahead of time to effectively maximize your releases. Ask your mix engineer to provide you with album stems as well as non-vocal versions of the song(s) and have your alternative mixes mastered at the same time as your primary track. Also ensure that your visual artist provides you with working files, Photoshop elements, and fonts, as per your agreement.*

In our *Record Label Marketing Strategies* online course, we have an in-depth module solely dedicated to this topic. Learn more at **otherrecordlabels.com/courses**

PART FOUR
CONCLUSION

Conclusion

Throughout this book, there are more than 150 practical, didactic tips, strategies, and recommended resources. This is important to note, because success in marketing does not come from a singular action, but from the compounding effects of many small ones.

Don't underestimate this cumulative power of small improvements. You may feel miles away from the record labels you admire but you won't get to where they are with one giant leap - but you can with multiple small steps forward. Your goal of having a sustainable record label is possible if you view these strategies as incremental improvements.

Developing a sustainable, effective marketing plan for your record label is the goal. Each tiny accomplishment provides micro-moments of positive reinforcement. This process will take time, anything great takes time. Be consistent, persistent, and implement as many of these strategies as possible.

Record labels exist to serve music fans and the music makers. Put all your marketing efforts through this filter. Bring value, respect the art, design with empathy, and create a vibrant community for artists and music fans to come together.

Record Label Marketing - FAQs

Here is a list of some of the common marketing questions I hear from folks in our record label community. Some of these questions have been answered in the pages above, but I thought it would be helpful to consolidate them together in one place.

How much does it cost to promote a new record?

I suppose it's possible to say that it can cost "nothing" but that would probably limit your marketing abilities and your distribution reach. But it's worth noting that, at the very least, you can upload music for free on Bandcamp or Soundcloud and use word-of-mouth and social media to promote your record.

On a more realistic level, distributing and promoting a new full-length record with a music publicist may cost anywhere between $500 - $10,000.

Should I release a single, EP, or full length?

I tend to think of these three formats as a natural evolution for a new artist. It is always best to test the waters with a single, perhaps a few singles. After you've established your artist profile on DSPs (Digital Service

Providers) – and learned what your audience enjoys – you can compile a few old songs and new songs into a new EP. Finally, a full-length record is something an artist should work towards, perhaps a year or two into their career launch.

Keep in mind that each of these three release levels require a greater amount of promotional attention. A full-length album comes with a more arduous marketing process that can include a publicist, manufacturing, multiple pre-release singles, a tour, and album merchandise.

Do I need to have our releases professionally mastered?

Music tech has come a long way, and you technically don't need to have your music mastered. You can upload your songs to DistroKid or CDBaby or Bandcamp whether they are mastered or not (it is reported that Spotify enacts a basic amount of volume leveling to all songs). Having said that, there's nothing quite like a professionally mastered release. A great mastering engineer takes into consideration all the various listening platforms that your audience may use. This helps the music sound best on any device and on any format.

Should a record label cover all marketing costs?

Yes, this is most common. However, it is best that you come to an agreement that is most comfortable for you and the artist. Commonly, marketing costs would be considered "recoupable" which means that the label is paid back for these expenses from all initial revenue until their investment has been "recouped." Some artists would prefer to financially contribute to the marketing expenses of their new release in order to minimize the amount of recoupables that their new release would owe to the record label.

There is no right or wrong answer, just ensure it is done fairly, and that every party understands the arrangement before any money has been spent.

How do I get my music on Spotify playlists?

At the time of writing this, the only way to get on to an official Spotify playlist is to use the Spotify for Artists portal to pitch your new singles. This should be done 2-6 weeks prior to release day, and you should have a well thought out pitch and artist bio prepared for when you are submitting a new song.

In addition to official Spotify editorial playlists, there are also third-party playlists that are often just as impactful as official playlists. To get on one of these playlists, you have to find out how they accept submissions. In some cases, you can email the curators directly (or DM them on social media). Some third-party playlists have their own submission portals on their website (Indiemono, AlexRainbirdMusic) and some playlists utilize tools like SubmitHub to manage their submissions.

Are traditional marketing methods (print, paid ads, etc.) still relevant?

A lot of these methods are far less effective than they used to be. However, for that reason, they may be less expensive than they used to be. The problem with a lot of traditional advertising methods is that they are often too broad to have any targeted impact. This means that if you buy a newspaper ad advertising a new release from a death metal artist, you could be paying to have this ad put in front of people who have no interest in death metal.

(That said, I've always thought it would be fun to rent a local billboard to advertise one of my new releases... Maybe one day.)

Should I pay a service to get my music on playlists?

Absolutely not. There are black market services that will charge you $50-$100 and guarantee a bulk number of streams. You may think this is a good investment to help your artist look legitimate, but the fact is that this will throw up serious red flags with Spotify, and it may get the artist blacklisted on their platform, or at worst, banned altogether. There are a few legitimate websites that aggregate data about playlists and their curators. Some of these websites charge a fee (Playlist Push, SubmitHub, Chartmetric) and provide contact information and listener data on a swath of official and unofficial Spotify playlists. The purpose of these tools is to find relevant and authentic playlists that you can build relationships with who you think would appreciate your releases.

How do I get the press to read my press releases?

Build relationships with these journalists and curators. Some of them get more than a hundred emails a day! Respect their time and respect how inundated they may be. Keep your pitches organized so you know who you contacted, when you contacted them and what the result of the pitch was. It is also important that you don't dismiss smaller, up-and-coming blogs. Blogs, DJs, and playlisters with smaller followings can still contribute to an overall successful PR campaign. Furthermore, some of them will eventually grow their platform into something much larger and they will appreciate the relationship they have with the artists and labels who supported them in their early days.

What is a music publicist, and do I need to hire one?

A music publicist is someone who will "pitch" your album or single to their press contacts. A good publicist can leverage their industry contacts to help get your releases to a wider audience. However, you often get what you pay for. You can expect a publicist to cost anywhere between $500-$5000 for a month-long campaign. The average PR campaign should cost you approximately $2000, but keep in mind that a publicist can't (and shouldn't) guarantee press coverage. Music is still subjective, and blogs and curators will only write about music they believe in. Try your hand at handling the PR campaigns for your first couple of releases to give you an idea of how it works and the effort that goes into pitching a record to the press. Once you get to know what's involved, you'll be in a better position to subcontract out parts of the campaign to someone stronger in certain areas of promotion than you are.

Should I invest in Facebook/Instagram/Google Ads?

The short answer is no. These are becoming more and more expensive and less and less effective. Audiences are programmed to ignore web ads, and I've never heard of a music fan saying they discovered their favorite band by way of a web banner. It is more effective to use more native and personable approaches to reaching listeners. Targeted ads seem like a good idea because platforms like Meta make it so easy to trial a campaign, but this carpet-bombing approach is very rarely effective and almost always expensive.

Other Record Labels Podcast
The Art and Culture of Running a Record Label

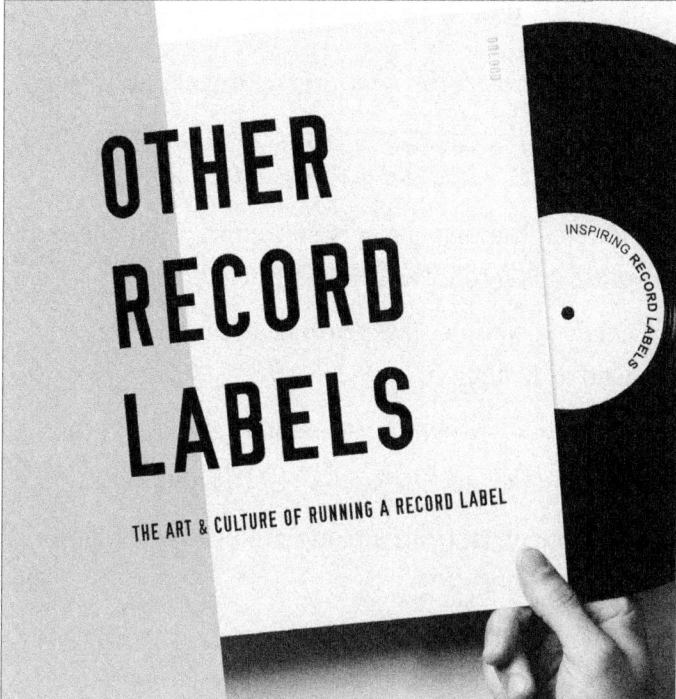

Listen to interviews and insights from today's independent record labels, including Sub Pop Records, Asthmatic Kitty Records, Mute Records, Ghostly International, Z Tapes, 6131 Records, Asian Man Records, Jagjaguar, and more!

Listen wherever you get your podcasts.

otherrecordlabels.com

Outside-the-Box Marketing Ideas

- Sending postcards announcing the album release
- Selling a short-run of an upcoming single on 7" vinyl, before it is released digitally
- Sending the first 3 songs of an upcoming album to press a few months prior to release
- Offering sample packs or mix stems as a free or paid download
- Release an instrumental version of the album
- Release an acoustic version of the album
- Have an artist from a completely different genre remix a song
- Submit the album art to Instagram accounts and blogs that showcase great graphic design
- Submit the artist's press photos to an Instagram account that showcases fashion
- Ask an Instagram influencer to use your song in one of their posts
- Submit your music to app developers to use as background music

- Run a contest or a giveaway
- Sell an album package that includes a personal performance via Skype
- Release a B-sides EP
- Release an artist-commentary version of the album
- Create behind-the-scenes content while the band is in the studio
- Interview the various people involved in making the record (mix engineer, photographer, graphic designer)
- Have the artist create a podcast with each episode focusing on each of their songs
- Put up posters around town advertising the new record
- Rent out a billboard to promote the new record

About the Author

Scott Orr is the host of *Other Record Labels*, a podcast about the art and culture of running a record label. Scott also runs Other Songs, a label he started in 2010. He lives and works in Ontario, Canada. He has two kids, and one of them is his favorite.

Instagram: @otherrecordlabels, @scott.orr

PART FIVE
ADDITIONAL RESOURCES

Additional Resources from *Other Record Labels*

Managing Royalties
otherrecordlabels.com/royalties

Music Publishing 101
otherrecordlabels.com/publishing

Reviewing Your Test Pressings
otherrecordlabels.com/testpressings

How to Make Cassette Tapes
otherrecordlabels.com/tapes

Sample Recording Contract
otherrecordlabels.com/recording-contract-template

Book Recommendations for Record Labels
otherrecordlabels.com/books

Bandcamp Resources
otherrecordlabels.com/bandcamp

Sync Licensing Resources
otherrecordlabels.com/sync

Pressing Vinyl Records
otherrecordlabels.com/vinyl

Release Schedule

ARTIST	TITLE	RELEASE DATE

Release Schedule

ARTIST	TITLE	RELEASE DATE

Contact List

PUBLICATION/COMPANY	NAME	CONTACT INFO	NOTES

Branding

NAME CHOICES	SOCIAL AVAILABILITY	URL AVAILABILITY	TRADEMARK CONFLICTS

LOGO CHECKLIST

- [ ] JPG
- [ ] EPS (Vector)
- [ ] Transparent (PNG)
- [ ] Black & White Version
- [ ] Layered Art Files
- [ ] Legibility
- [ ] _____

BRAND CHECKLIST

- [ ] Brand Color(s)
- [ ] Brand Font(s)
- [ ] Logo Usage Guidelines
- [ ] Label Motto/Slogan
- [ ] Brand Preferred Username
- [ ] Socials/URLs Secured
- [ ] _____

LABEL DOCUMENTS CHECKLIST

- [ ] Letterhead
- [ ] Return Address Stickers
- [ ] Invoice Template
- [ ] Receipt Template
- [ ] New Artist Info Sheet
- [ ] Staff Contact List
- [ ] _____

ADDITIONAL BRANDING NOTES _____

_____

_____

_____

_____

_____

_____

_____

_____

Notes

Notes

Notes

Notes

PRODUCTIVITY PLANNER BY **OTHER RECORD LABELS**

26 Week Organizational Journal

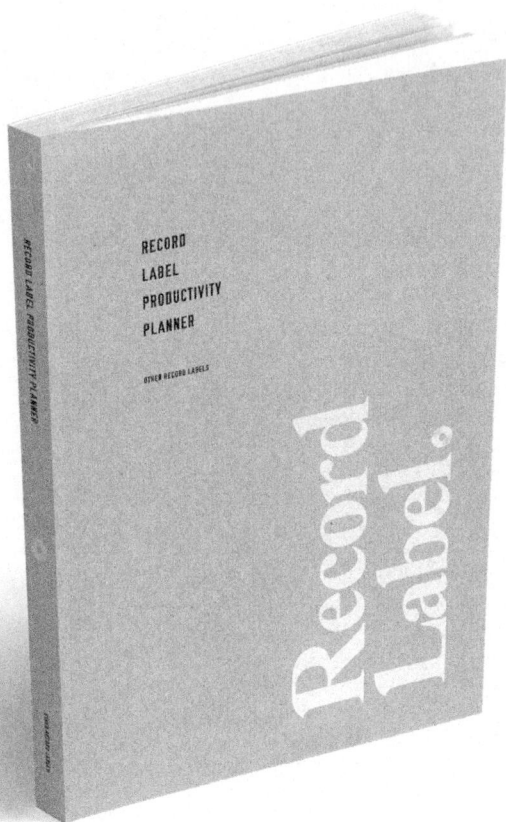

otherrecordlabels.com/book

MICRO BOOKS BY **OTHER RECORD LABELS**

Single-Subject Music Industry Guides

otherrecordlabels.com/book

otherrecordlabels.com

Online Courses for Record Labels

otherrecordlabels.com/courses

Printed in Great Britain
by Amazon